WAS IT WORTH IT?
Recollections
of a
Village Mayor

A Political History *by*
Former Port Chester Mayor
Peter Iasillo

1970-1993

Written 1994-1998

iUniverse, Inc.
New York   Bloomington

Was It Worth It?
Recollections of a Village Mayor

iUniverse books may be ordered through booksellers or by contacting:

iUniverse
1663 Liberty Drive
Bloomington, IN 47403
www.iuniverse.com
1-800-Authors (1-800-288-4677)

Because of the dynamic nature of the Internet, any Web addresses or links contained in this book may have changed since publication and may no longer be valid. The views expressed in this work are solely those of the author and do not necessarily reflect the views of the publisher, and the publisher hereby disclaims any responsibility for them.

ISBN: 978-1-4401-3560-6 (pbk)
ISBN: 978-1-4401-3561-3 (ebk)

Printed in the United States of America

iUniverse rev. date: 4/27/2009

WAS IT WORTH IT?

FORWARD

Why would a former village Mayor want to write a book about his years in office? Shouldn't he rest on his laurels? Maybe it's ego. Maybe it's his legacy to his family and the future generations of the village that he loved and served. Possibly it is to remind the outside world that local elected officials, at the lowest rung of the ladder in regards to politics and government, can be the hardest job there is. Never do we hear of the person at the bottom who continually serves his constituency on a one-to-one basis, upfront and not protected by aides or assistants. The guy or gal who must write their own press releases, their own speeches, one who is continually on the firing line and must respond by his or her wits and intelligence, knowledge, and sense of recollection.

The writing of this book is to share a history of small village politics and what the Mayor of a small community must contend with in order to stay one step ahead of his troubled constituency.

The contents of this book will cover local town officials, their constituents and citizens of various political parties that I recall, all of whose ideas, considered good or bad, have either failed or succeeded in influencing local officials in making Village policy. There are many public officials whose stories are not included but who, by their dedication, influenced their own constituency. Of these bold, conscientious officials, I include Mayor Al DelVecchio, Mayor

Phil Zeggarelli, Mayor Thom Serrani, Village Manager Lowell Tooely, and Supervisor Pat Angarano. These men represent what all local officials should emulate. I hope I can somehow stimulate interest and bring enjoyment to my readers.

LOYALTY: "Constant and faithful in any relation implying trust or confidence: bearing true allegiance to constituted authority: professing or indicative of faithful devotion."

DEDICATED TO

My wife Gloria, who served as my conscience and whose advice I should have taken on some issues, especially late in my political career, whose love and dedication kept me going ahead.

My family, whose love I cherish and who, because of my years in public service, I neglected on too many occasions and their problems that needed my attention.

My best friend, hero and advisor, my dad, Casper, Sr., who was truthful and loving to me.

My father-in-law, Ralph Sementini, whose pride in my public service was boundless. The Village of Port Chester, a community in transition that has suffered from a negative image that is not deserved.

CONTENTS

ANTHONY RENDE

If there was ever a citizen of Port Chester who spoke with great eloquence, dignity and love for his community and country, it was Anthony Rende. In all my years of public service, he was the only person who could stir many emotions as he orated his love for Port Chester and the U.S.A. "Tony" Rende moved everyone as he presented his thoughts on various subjects that aroused him. His oratory could bring tears to your eyes and make you think twice about a decision to be made by the Board of Trustees. His love for his fellow man, no matter what race, color, or religion was quite evident to anyone who heard him speak. He was fearless and did not think of anything that might befall him politically as he addressed the multitude.

Proud of his Italian heritage, Tony Rende also loved America with such fervor that he shamed those citizens born in the U.S.A. who took their citizenship for granted. His story of his entering the U.S.A. at thirteen years of age; a very young man landing at Ellis Island in winter, clad in short pants, all alone and wide eyed at the sight of the Statue of Liberty and scared of being asked questions by Ellis Island inspectors is truly a story of awe and anxiety. He did not know the language and even feared being sent back to Italy. It is a tale of a courageous young man whose love for the U.S.A. never diminished. Movies are made of such stories.

Tony Rende volunteered for many committees for various events and celebrations in his Village ranging from historical and patriotic events to church and service groups. His generosity was legendary. Anyone approaching him selling chances for any worthy function would see him buying more tickets than anyone else. At functions where the hat was passed, he was always the first one to contribute. With his lovely wife Louise, they personified the best in human beings. One thing Tony Rende wanted in his lifetime was to serve his Village as an elected official. He ran for public office once on an Independent line and lost.

But his loss never deterred him from his goal to see that Port Chester received the best in development. Tony got his wish however, to serve through his son Joseph, who in 1989 was elected a Village Trustee. The night Joseph was sworn in we saw Tony Rende at his most eloquent as he spoke of Port Chester, the U.S.A., the Village Board, his son, and the American dream. There wasn't a dry eye in the courtroom that night. The love he had for his son and family, and Joseph's hugging and kissing his dad was really an emotional high. It certainly brought tears to my eyes as my thoughts turned to my own dad, deceased, who never saw me sworn into office as Mayor.

Certainly Tony Rende was a man with a big heart and a profound love for Port Chester.

ARGELIO RODRIGUEZ

In the mid to late 1970's there rose in the Village of Port Chester a new, strong minority voice, that being the Spanish Coalition, which would play an important part in future Village elections. Two people who recognized their voting potential was Dom Pierro, and a Cuban-American who was the prime organizer and leader of the Port Chester Latinos, Argelio Rodriguez. Dom Pierro, because of his fluency with the Spanish language saw his business as an attorney increase as more and more of his clients were Hispanics. Dom saw in these people the same traits of early Italian-Americans, that loyalty to America and the work ethic; no hand outs, but find a job and work hard. In those 1970's there were two Cuban-American clubs, the "Circulo Cubano" and the "Los '70". The Circulo Cubano was more in tune with Republican ideas while the Los '70 were more oriented to the Democrats.

Argelio, the president of the Circulo Cubano, was a masterful organizer and a fiery speaker. When speaking stimulated and brought his audience to a fever pitch, he won out for the Latino vote and the Los '70 Club was disbanded. With his wife Mary, Argelio slowly but surely put together an organization that would have great significance in those Village elections of the 1980's. I was probably the greatest recipient of their organization as I started out in 1980 as Mayor. It was a delight to see how Argelio would plan each election, getting in record numbers new Hispanic registrants and then seeing to it that they voted on Election Day. Our friendship really blossomed in the mid

3

1970's. This was at a time when the influx of Latinos in Port Chester really started. It was also at this time that the Circulo Cubano Club asked that a small plot of Village land be set aside to erect a bust of Jose Marti, the revered person in all Cuba, who brought democracy to the island. Argelio wielded his influence with Dom Pierro and then to Joe Dzaluk, Dan LaDore, and myself. We all knew that this would be controversial idea because the Village, in general, was still somewhat skeptical of what good Cuban-Americans had done or would do for Port Chester.

To the credit of all those mentioned above, the land, a small triangular piece at the intersection of Haseco and Glen Avenues, was agreed to as the place to dedicate the bronze bust. With money they raised by their hard work, under an overcast sky, the bust was unveiled. It still wasn't without controversy as acts of vandalism damaged the bust several times, but through Argelio's leadership no acts of retribution occurred

Argelio's skills at organizing publicity, or, as he would say "propaganda", reached both county and state levels of Republicanism. The one thing that diminished his effectiveness was his hatred for Communism and as a result he resigned from those appointive organizations in which he envisaged as Socialist or non-republican. He was the prime mover in seeing to it that his fellow Hispanics took advantage of the school system and organized night classes to teach the English language. He encouraged service to the Village by suggesting names of Hispanics to serve on various Village Commissions. When political rallies were to be held, the Port Chester Republican Party now included a special Latino rally at the Polish Hall where Argelio brought together literally hundreds of his people to meet and listen to Republican candidates. These rallies were always an enormous success. It was a delight to see him react when things went right, like winning an election, by putting his thumb and two fingers together and in a snapping motion indicate that things were great or that his election district won. As I continued to be re-elected Mayor, I had many early morning meetings with Argelio at the Mayor's office as we planned strategy, talked of "propaganda", or his appeal to me to help some of his needy friends. Through his efforts, my administration finally saw to it that there was a Spanish interpreter in the Village Court and had many ordinances dealing with housing translated into Spanish.

Unfortunately, Argelio was not a healthy person. His heart was failing and in 1989, shortly after my re-election, he passed away.

His dream of a young Hispanic being elected to public office never came to pass although his son Nelson attempted to be elected in both town and school elections but lost.

Ironically, that small patch of triangular land on which the bust of Jose Marti stands was dedicated in August 1989 as Argelio Rodriguez Park, to memorialize the man who did so much for not only Port Chester Hispanics but the entire Village. The last election he participated in was in 1989, my re-election. Although ill, he told me that he was working to see that he got me re-elected. I will never forget the talk we had that day before the election and he said to me in his broken English, "Pete, you will win, I guarantee it." By his death, I lost another loyal friend.

ARNOLD BERNFELD

One of the most faithful and lovable persons to serve Village government was Arnold Bernfeld. Arnold was a person whose loyalty to the Republican Party and to me were unwavering. Arnold served diligently and with pride as Port Chester's Village Treasurer for over 15 years. His honesty was never questioned and the efforts on behalf of our Village were boundless. A true gentleman with a great sense of humor, Arnold was loved and respected by everyone: Republicans, Democrats, and the whole community; except for possibly Sam Terenzi, a Village Trustee. Arnold's close friendship to me, I believe, infuriated Sam. Sam referred to Arnold as "my stooge." Arnold and I would laugh at this childish remark.

Arnold burst upon the political scene in 1970. Joe Dzaluk won a great victory over the incumbent Mayor Al Nencetti and with Dan LaDore and myself achieving victories as Trustees, the Board, now with a 5 to 2 Republican majority, met to appoint the various people to serve in Village government. Irv Granowitz was considered for the post of Village Treasurer. Mr. Granowitz declined the appointment since he felt he could not devote the time necessary to fill that post. The entire Board of Republicans was stymied. Who was out there to take this important position? I think Rose Margolies suggested to Mayor Dzaluk the name of Arnold Bernfeld.

Those of us on the Board didn't know Arnold however, as soon as we learned of his education and professional background we knew that he was the ideal person to be our Village Treasurer.

Arnold was held in high esteem by those in the accounting profession and was also very active in our Village with the Boy Scouts, achieving Scouting's highest award, the honor of the Silver Beaver. He was also active with the Volunteer Ambulance Corp. as their unpaid accountant, the Port Chester High School Band Parents Association and many more charitable and religious organizations. I did not know Arnold. When I first met him I was very impressed by his appearance with his bold mustache and equally bold shock of gray hair. He really looked like a tough cookie.

It was only years later as we became close friends that I realized that he was a real gentleman, concerned and caring for all people and loved and respected throughout the Village. He was a real pussycat.

As the Republicans took over the reins of government in May, 1970, the plan as outlined by Mayor Dzaluk, was to keep everything low key until we could assess those problems left by the past administration. On May 5, 1970, we were sworn into office. Less than two weeks later the headlines had read, "BERNFELD CLAIMS PORT CHESTER IN THE RED." Then days later the headlines read, "TREASURERS DISPUTE VILLAGE DEBT." With that, all plans for keeping things low key vanished. This action by Arnold of coming forward with the facts left me with the impression that he was a gutsy and honest person. Arnold and I would continually laugh and talk about those headlines. I personally presented him with a framed copy of both headlines at a dinner on October 25, 1991 where Arnold was honored Republican of the Year in Port Chester.

Things went along pretty well in the ensuing months. Arnold stated that the Village had a $237,000 deficit as confirmed by a New York State audit, and then the headlines on January 5, 1971, even bolder than the May 1970 headlines stated, "BERNFELD: PORT CHESTER IS HALF MILLION IN RED, FORMER BOARD BLAMED." Arnold did it again. The argument went on and on. How much was Port Chester in debt?

Since I was Chairman of the Finance Committee for the Village, Arnold and I became even closer friends because of our dealing with the Village budget.

As time went on, Arnold's position as Treasurer was ended several times as Democrats became the majority party. Naturally, when that happened Arnold was out. That was part of politics, and those of us who served in public office realized this, especially Arnold. Arnold and his wife Sonya became very close friends with Gloria and I. It was a friendship that Gloria and I really cherished. It was a friendship of real happiness as we traveled every year to some tourist haven in the Barbados, Bermuda, Mexico, or to foreign lands in Europe. There were also the times we traveled together to the Conference of Mayors educational seminars and schools.

`One particularly funny experience included an evening when Gloria and I, Sonya and Arnold, Brien and Bea McMahon, Jack and Donna Munnick, Donna and Fritz Falanka and Sandy were playing "Trivial Pursuit." It is a game that requires concentration and remembering many varied facts. Arnold and Sonya were not doing very well. During the middle of the game Arnold decided he needed to go to the bathroom and have a bowel movement. We all laughed because he told us he was leaving for that reason. Well, as luck would have it when the roll of the dice by Sonya and the card with the question came up, Sonya didn't have an answer. She then proceeded to yell to Arnold, in the bathroom, the question. Arnold quickly answered correctly. Sonya again rolled the dice, picked the card with the questions and yelled to Arnold. Again, Arnold answered quickly and correctly. This went on several times. When Arnold finally left the bathroom, he was again stymied by the questions and couldn't answer any more questions correctly. He reasoned and told us that while in the bathroom he had the opportunity to clear his brain. At that remark, we all burst out laughing.

There had been years of a strong friendship which also endured sadness as our parents, Gloria's dad and my dad, and Sonya's parents passed away. We also saw our children grow up, and even consoled each other in seeking to find answers to problems that arose in all our families. In all my years in public office Arnold Bernfeld had been a true friend. I read somewhere, "It is great to have friends when one is young, but indeed it is still more so when you are getting old. When we are young, friends are like everything else, a matter of course. In the old days we know what it means to have them." Well, I certainly do. I'm proud to have had as my friend, Arnold Bernfeld. Sadly, I had to give the eulogy at Arnold's untimely death. Again I had lost a close, dear friend.

CHRISTOPHER PIERRO

As one reads each short statement of those who participated in any way or added in any way some attitude or work to me on my administration, I continually refer to one important word. That word is <u>loyalty.</u> Any public official, especially a Mayor, must have a cadre of people who work and assist him or her, especially from the primary opposition, in this case, the Democrats. However, more people also appear on the scene and those are the backstabbers, those that work underhandedly to seek power at the expense of anyone, including the Mayor, of those that helped these people achieve success in the public arena. These are, unfortunately, the egotists, bent on getting ahead at any expense no matter how dishonorable they can be.

One young man, full of energy and vitality who continually sought to help me was Christopher Pierro. In the early 1980's, Chris, through hard work and an aptitude to remember names and an extraordinary amount of energy, saw his business grow by leaps and bounds. His business became so successful that he started to participate and use his energies in local Village elections as well as County and State elections. His particular talent lay in his ability to arrange and institute the raising of money for the local Republican campaigns. I remember distinctly, as I prepared to run for re-election in 1982, the question as to how to raise money for an effective campaign. Chris boldly came forward and said he would raise the money needed.

He arranged for the first time a fundraising party with a ticket to a surf and turf dinner priced at $100 per person. This was unheard of in 1982. You might sell tickets for a political campaign on the County or State level at $100, but never for a local Village campaign. There were some of those Republican leaders who scoffed at the idea and couldn't wait for Chris to fall flat on his face. However, as Chris predicted, the party was a huge success and thousands of dollars were raised and Chris was recognized as a premier fundraiser to raise election money. He did this for every Village campaign, gathering in the dollars needed to win elections. His efforts were never fully recognized and, in fact, those same people who Chris helped were the same ones that criticized him and in general never fully appreciated the things he did for them. Chris was a generous individual, almost to a fault. These people who criticized Chris were the same ones who sought out Chris for free tickets to ball games and political parties.

From 1982 on, Chris and I became friendlier and he confided in me many of his business and personal problems, seeking my advice and counsel. His friendship with me led to his being slowly but surely ostracized by those same Republicans he had helped. I recognized this and told Chris that he should be careful of his friendships and what he talked of. That was one of Chris' biggest drawbacks. He placed his faith in everyone and had a tendency to reveal any and all information he knew of, no matter what the subject was. His so-called friends tolerated him because he was financially successful but when the crash of 1987 on Wall Street hit and his business started to decline, Chris started to see the changes. Those who talked quietly and behind his back now became more open to ridiculing Chris and his dad, County Legislator Dom. It created tension within his family as Chris found himself pulled in two directions, by his family and by the so-called buddies. It was quite a time in Chris' life when he was literally befuddled. He tried to find the reasons why his political friends would do or say such cruel things

Fortunately, Chris' strong and loving wife Maria also saw what was going on and cautioned Chris in his dealings with all people. She supported him and would fight for him if need be. Chris made some drastic changes in his business. He had to, as it was suffering terribly by the declining real estate market. These changes worked and started to bear fruit, and his business started to rebound. His ambition to run for elected office or serve as a member of a commission was usually rebuffed. In fact, there were times when even I cautioned him about getting involved as I felt it would affect his business and his dad who was at the time our County Legislator.

A famous quote stated, "There are few, if any, traits in which ability alone is sufficient. Needed also are *loyalty, sincerity, enthusiasm, and team play.*"

This statement certainly personifies Chris Pierro, a real loyal friend who, because of our friendship, bore the brunt of criticism by many hypocritical so-called friends.

DOMINICK "MIMI" CATALANO

If there was one individual that provided me with laughs, assistance, headaches, and advice (good and bad), was a smallish 5'5" bundle of energy named Dom "Mimi" Catalano.

My adventures with Mimi started almost from the first day I was sworn into office as a Village Trustee, back in May 1970. Mimi is a particularly gifted individual with the knowledge of carpentry, cabinet making, plumbing, electrical work, etc., but in 1970 he was a Democrat that worked against my election bid for Village Trustee. I won that election and as was the practice in those early 1970's, to the victor belonged the spoils, in this case Republicans get hired, not Democrats. In Mimi's case I pushed hard to hire Mimi as the Village of Port Chester handyman. My efforts proved successful but I created such a stir and furor in the Republican Party that I wondered whether I made the correct decision to push for Mimi's employment. Well the record will show that I did make the right decision. However, I soon found out that Mimi would always cause problems for either the Republican Party or the Democratic Party in his years employed by the Village. His smallish stature and uncanny way of knowing what was going on in the Village assisted me in many, many ways. I sometimes felt that Mimi should have been a CIA agent. It was fantastic the knowledge he possessed about the inner workings of Port Chester. He has his personal struggles with his immediate supervisors and/or political enemies which required my getting involved because, in most cases, he was being beset upon because of his friendship and loyalty to me.

The thing I will remember Mimi for is the laughs he gave me, like the time he nailed Sam Serio's chair to the floor, upsetting Sam very much and following this up with phony phone calls to Sam from phony corporations about parking meters and to see Sam react with such a businesslike manner. There was also the time he had Sam Serio talking to phony heating engineers regarding the heating unit in Sam's office. Seeing Sam react with such seriousness was very comical. Or the time Mimi removed the speaking piece from Sam's phone and then Sam receiving phone calls and yelling into the phone because the people on the other end were telling Sam they couldn't hear him. These and other comical antics kept me laughing for many years.

There were also the ways that Mimi contrived stories that really confused his assistant Frank Gabriele. Frank always wondered whether or not he should believe such wild, inventive tales he had to listen to. Frank also had a condition I guess you would describe as being "goosey." Merely a touch to his backside would have Frank leap forward to heights of at least a foot yelling in wild violent screams was quite a thing to behold. Mimi would find ways to touch Frank whether it be with a ruler, a screwdriver, a pencil, a stick; anything that was near was used and Frank always reacted in the same way. I will never forget Dom "Mimi" Catalano. Today he is a changed man who prays and attends church regularly. His life has changed with marital and other financial problems, however, he still phones me regularly and provides me with funny stories and recites rhymes and poems that he now writes and has won many literary awards for. He amazingly still knows what is going on in Port Chester. Yes, he should have been a CIA agent. Well, in a way he is CIA, Comical Italian American.

EDWARD M. SALTZMAN

A wise man stated, "Small kindnesses, small courtesies, small considerations, habitually practiced in our daily business, give greater charm to the character than the display of great talent and accomplishments." Oh how this statement describes Eddy Saltzman. I have never in my many years of political life met a more kindly and considerate individual than Eddy Saltzman. I first had the opportunity to meet Eddy in 1974 when then Mayor Joe Dzaluk recommended Ed for the position of Corporation Counsel. From the very first time I met him, I saw in Eddy traits that in some ways paralleled my Dad's.

His demeanor was quiet and subdued, his patience was endless, his reaction to problems was restrained and well thought out, and there was never a shred of vindictiveness in his whole body. As Ed pursued the job as Corporation Counsel, it was clear at the beginning, at least to me, that his background and training was not geared to the numerous tasks that beset a Corporation Counsel. Yet even without this background, he became a great Corporation Counsel.

When I became Mayor, the first person I wanted on my team was Eddy Saltzman. We became a close-knit duo. We met almost every evening in his office and discussed issues that led me to make important decisions that dramatically changed Port Chester. Our discussions about the importance of having a full time attorney in the employ of the Village led me to the bringing forward and enacting of the law creating the office of Village Attorney. His actions along with two dear friends, Dom Pierro and Sam Lerner, brought about the review and subsequent recommendation to hiring George O'Hanlon whose service to the Village and my administration proved invaluable. Through our many meetings and discussions, I learned from Ed that every problem that came forward to the Mayor and Board of Trustees was solvable. He continually stressed patience and quiet diplomacy, advice that proved so valuable to me as I pressed forward with ideas and issues that were, for our community, far-reaching and controversial.

His advice on going ahead with the Southport and Kingsport Housing Developments proved right, as they shortly became the catalyst to bigger and better things for Port Chester. The decisions on these two developments were politically difficult decisions, but they helped us go ahead with the federal government on many more developments using many dollars from federal and county grants that we received. The millions of dollars Port Chester received outdistanced any other community in Westchester and indeed the United States. Eddy continually cautioned me against being vindictive and attempting to get even with those who slandered me by merely stating, "Do you want to be like those people and get into the dirt and mud?" I often think back to this statement and can appreciate the advice and counsel he gave me. I can remember only one time he became angry, and it was after I became Mayor at my second term and re-appointed my dedicated, loyal, and competent friends to important offices in my administration. This action prompted a citizen to make remarks in writing questioning the honesty of the persons appointed. This infuriated Eddy and for the first time he took an action to sue the person who made such a slanderous statement.

But as Eddy so often counseled me, he accepted an apology from the person who wrote the statement and forgot the whole matter and the lawsuit.

I often think back to the good times and really difficult times Ed and I weathered through. Like the grand jury investigation of myself, Eddy, and other officials in regards to our supposed attempt to abrogate the civil rights of a weekly newspaper and our difficulty in coming forth with a contract with the Bredero Corporation for the development of our downtown harbor at Fox Island. I also remember the good times we had attending Giants football games, being transported to the Meadowlands in a limo and the party and dinner afterwards with friends and spouses at Eddy's home.

On September 8, 1982, my friend Ed Saltzman died of a heart attack and diabetes at the young age of 56. For me it was a great loss and I remember sobbing as I served as a pallbearer at his funeral. Eddy will be remembered in

Port Chester. I saw to it that the Kingsport Housing Development had his name and a suitable plaque installed in his honor. I surely miss this devoted friend and ally and remember one final bit of advice he gave me.

He said, "Peter, don't hope for a Board of Trustees with all Republicans, it will give you problems." Eddy was again right with his advice as I learned many years later.

FRANK J. MOKRZSKI

Try to picture a short, portly fellow literally waddling to the microphone to address the Board of Trustees. His haircut is short yet still tousled and his pants are below his belly button. His t-shirt is ill fitting, which naturally reveals his belly button. With this you have Frank Moe-krit-ski. Frank was an individual who sporadically attended Board meetings, probably only when a full moon was in the sky or so it seemed. He frequently made statements during public meetings not in any way related to the subject and it was comical at most times to listen to his remarks. In the early years of my mayoralty I became very agitated with Frank.

He was forever either interrupting other speakers at the microphone or murmuring quite loudly to himself as he sat which became very distracting to everyone. This type of behavior frequently precipitated arguments between Frank, the speaker, and the Board members. It got to such a point that for a time I would never recognize Frank to speak at these hearings, which in itself was illegal. At public hearing I by law had to recognize him, but for three months I wouldn't allow Frank to address the board. Whenever Frank saw me in the Village he would plead with me to allow him to speak but I told him for three months I would not. So, for three months, the Board did not hear any vocalizing from Frank Moe-krit-ski.

When Frank came to the microphone no one really knew or could comprehend what he would bring up for discussion. He had special nicknames for me in particular. He referred to me on various occasions as Mussolini, El Duce, Khrushchev, the dictator, etc. He would take great delight at public hearings when Judge Bruno Gioffre would be representing a client to accuse the Judge as being a crooked Judge, of being on the take, and other such inflammatory statements. In the late 1980's he increased his name calling to include Trustees, which really agitated them, probably because they didn't understand Frank as I found out later.

Frank, to my way of thinking, in his own disjointed way was a decent man. His thoughts on the Village, it's elected and appointed officials varied from meeting to meeting.

As an example, the meeting in question centered on code enforcement and over crowding in apartments in violation of our housing code. Frank rose to address the Board, waddling to the microphone and in a soft, gentle voice related to us how he had allowed a Salvadoran family to live, seven in a room, in his apartment house for a few weeks because, "they had nowhere to go." He said he was being humane by letting them stay in the room. The reaction to his statement was first loud laughter, then castigation by Board members. When he then questioned us about the amount of fines connected with over crowding, he quickly, before getting an answer, probably thought it was better to shut up at this point because he could see he was going to put himself in a hole. I learned later that he was served with housing violations.

The Judges in our court were so incensed by his down grading of their reputations that they referred his case to a Mamaroneck Village Court.

Sadly, in August 1990, Frank was indicted and found guilty of shooting and murdering one of his tenants and was sentenced to an extended jail term.

FRED "FRITZ" TEDESCO

As with any community, there is always a person who constantly personifies contradictory ideas and feelings that continually bring forward pessimistic and doomsday type opinions.

Such a person, who from the mid 1960's personified these negative opinions, was Fritz Tedesco. Fritz, along with his brother-in-law Rocky, frightened and intimidated many elected officials with a continuance of negative opinions it seemed on every progressive idea brought forth. In those late 1960's and throughout the 1970's, Fritz and Rocky appeared at school board and trustee meetings bringing with them copies of newspaper stories, their opinions of facts always indicating they seemed to know positively that they were right and the elected officials were wrong and not considerate of the taxpayer.

I first got to know Fritz during my initial 1970 campaign for Trustee. Fritz was an ardent supporter of our ticket, but most especially of Joe Dzaluk. He made fiery speeches on our behalf, sang Nelson Eddy songs, and related fact after fact. I must admit I was taken in by what I felt was a deep sincerity on his part to see our ticket elected. It was only after the election that I learned he was promised a job if we won and became a majority on the Board of Trustees. Sure enough we won and Fritz got his job with the Public Works Dept. Sadly to say, Fritz totally intimidated some Board members and even when we learned of his dismal record as an employee, nothing was done by the Republican leadership to bring Fritz into line. This particularly upset me because I saw my neighbor, Tony Scinto, demoted only because he was a registered Democrat, and nothing was done to Fritz, a political hack concerned only with his personal gratification.

The problem with Fritz continued for some time. It took some years for the Republican leadership to recognize the liabilities associated with being linked with Fritz and the Conservative Party. Republicans held many meetings as to how to find a way to rid the party of his influence.

Finally, an idea came forward to embarrass Fritz in such a way that he would quit. For all these years Fritz had felt the idea was mine. It was not. It was concocted by the late Dan LaDore: Fritz would be outfitted in white coveralls, push a cart with a painted white barrel, equipped with a push broom and shovel, and sweep the gutters of Port Chester. The idea worked. Fritz left.

I guess Fritz's greatest triumph came in 1979 when he, the Conservative Party, and the Concerned Citizens Committee banded together to endorse Bob Kancir for the vacant seat of Trustee Mike Pierro. It was ironic that Fritz was endorsing a candidate, against the person who possibly most aided and endorsed Fritz's ideas, Joe Dzaluk. No one really gave much hope to Bob Kancir's candidacy, but as had proved to be not the norm in Port Chester, Bob Kancir won the election. Naturally, Fritz took credit for the win, however, it was always felt that certain circumstances elected an Independent candidate. First, many people were tired of both political parties. Second, Bob Kancir was a popular and respected citizen. Third, the Concerned Citizens Committee under the leadership of Sal Lucente, really got the vote out and that was the main force in Bob's victory. My opinion, the Conservative Party of Port Chester, under Fritz's leadership, had given very little votes and support toward any candidate.

A bit of fresh air came into the Conservative Party when in the mid 1980's, Joe Dzaluk III, son of former Mayor Joe Dzaluk, took over as head of the Conservative Party. Things were coming into place. The new, bright leadership of the younger Joe Dzaluk saw a political resurgence of Republicans and Conservatives. Fiscal conservative responsibility and new, far reaching ideas on redevelopment blended together to make both political parties a real positive force for Port Chester. Unfortunately this blend was short lived as Joe Dzaluk, an IBM employee, was transferred to Germany and the leadership again went to Fritz Tedesco.

Elections come and go in Port Chester. There are still those politicians who court favor from Fritz and the Conservative Party. The politicians still bow down to him. I had never done so.

I was diametrically opposed to his ideas. I had proved in 10 elections that without the Conservative support I still came out victorious.

GAZEBO - CONCERTS IN THE PARK

In 1981, after being in office as Mayor for one year, I felt that there had to be some one event to not only emotionally stir Village residents but also bring into our Village, out-of-towners, to change their attitude toward Port Chester. Port Chester, unfortunately, still had a poor reputation that needed changing if it were to become a community that people wanted to live and work in.

Since I had started up the Council for the Arts and it was working out well, I needed a quality of life event that would be an annual event. My thoughts turned to music and concerts in the park. The idea of having an annual event, in the summer season, was a great way to market our Village. The idea was firmly in my mind and I was convinced that having concerts in the park was like hitting a home run. It certainly turned out to be a winning event. I reasoned that in the 1940's, concerts in the park brought many of our citizens and neighbors together, and a free event would be all the more reason for people to attend. But the Village needed a financial sponsor. Who could I turn to?

Pilot Pen Corporation, a corporation located in Port Chester at the time, fortunately had a dynamic Executive Vice President, Mr. Ron Shaw. A former nightclub entertainer, Ron Shaw recognized immediately what I was striving for in Port Chester. At a public function Ron asked me if Pilot Pen could do

21

anything to help our Village. That was my opening. I immediately posed the idea of summer concerts. Without hesitation he accepted the responsibility to have Pilot Pen financially sponsor the concerts. With the financing in place, I was ready to get the event started up. But I also reasoned that this first concert had to be a super special first concert. Draw an enormous crowd to the first concert and we could have the crowd return. What did I have to do?

The idea to really market this first concert came from Virginia and Andy Telesca. They said, "Why not invite retired Colonel Paul Weckesser, the person who was loved in Port Chester and the High School's former Musical Director and leader of the 1940's concerts?"

What a fantastic idea. We called Colonel Weckesser and he joyfully accepted. Pilot Pen arranged, free of charge, for his plane tickets and the Rye Town Hilton, through Mr. Perhelman, Manager, arranged for the Colonel's accommodation also free of charge. So now we were set for July 17, 1981, for the first of two scheduled concerts. Pilot Pen put up the financing, Colonel Weckesser would attend, our conductor, Jerry Sala, was all set. THE NEW YORK TIMES publicized the event. All we needed was good weather.

Friday, July 17, 1981, the weather was great. The crowd was spectacular. Over 1,500 people attended. We had a winner; my idea worked. Before the concert the Dixie Dandies entertained free of charge. The A.F.M. Local #38, through Peter Pugliese, assisted with the costs for the Union musicians. My heart was overjoyed that evening. I had accomplished what I wanted. My ego was also somewhat inflated because I hoped Village residents would always remember that Mayor Iasillo started it all.

Everything continued to go well in 1981 and 1982. From two concerts in 1981 and 1982 they increased to four concerts in 1983. I then figured that the band playing on platforms was not proper. What do we do? My idea was to build a gazebo to house the band. I had seen throughout New England how a gazebo added to the quality of life through this region of the United States. Clerk Richard Falanka and I pondered how big this gazebo should be? What would be the cost? How long would it take to build? We inspected gazebos in Pleasantville, New York and Stamford, Connecticut. They did not meet our idea of a super, great gazebo. It was then at a Rotary meeting that I approached Angelo LaBate, a local architect, to design a gazebo. However, I informed him that we had no funds to pay for an architect. After several meetings, Angelo agreed to design a super, special gazebo at no charge. However, we had to promise that he be given every opportunity to really use his imagination. I agreed and the result was a design beyond our dreams.

The final design for the gazebo is over 40 feet in width, features a star like shaped roof with a tongue and grooved ceiling, tubular steel columns and rails on a red brick foundation.

The gazebo combines the beauty of artistic design with the soundness of superior workmanship, and large enough to accommodate our entire 45 piece concert orchestra. But how do we pay an estimated $65,000 to build this magnificent structure? That's when the arm-twisting, cajoling, and pleading took place. For this project I was at my best in the begging department.

Every corporation I talked to was willing to help either by donating materials or labor or both. The Baker Corp. came through with the brick. Excavating was done by the DeCarlo brothers, Abe and Muzzy. Ron Luiso donated concrete. Vincent Sergi donated the steel supports, the steel railings from Bill Gasparini of the Post Road Iron Works, electrical fixtures from Patdo Electric, labor to install the fixtures from Joe Vitti at Brooksville Electric. The donation of lumber, roofing supplies, nails, etc. was interesting and funny. I went to Jack Kahan at Interstate Lumber and begged for the 2 X 4 materials, wood piers, etc. I told him that as a former Port Chester-ite, he would want to donate the materials.

I then pulled the clincher. I told him that Main Street Lumber in Port Chester was ready to donate it all if Jack Kahan would not. That did it. Jack Kahan would not hear of it. He stated, "Port Chester is my home town. I will donate all the lumber." Elated by this, I then proceeded to meet with Jerry Lombardi at Main Street Lumber. I told him I needed roofing tile, tarpaper, nails, sheeting boards, etc. I told him if he refused me, Jack Kahan of Interstate was ready to donate it. Of course, I was bluffing him. The result, Jerry Lombardi stated, "Hell he will, Main Street Lumber is a Port Chester business. Forget Jack Kahan and Interstate. We will donate the materials." The bluff worked and we had the lumber we needed.

The labor was an important part of the whole operation. With qualified people such as John Belfatto, Tony Fontana, and Tony Giuliani, the construction went forward. It was slow only because the labor was volunteer and we had to do much of it in the nighttime and on weekends. From start to finish it took about 15 months. But the results we saw were fantastic. Our Village Manager, Mike Ritchie, saw to it that whenever possible, Village personnel were transferred to help in the process.

I had already lined up Ed Baran, Tom Amendola, and Ed Pierson to volunteer the painting of the structure.

The really heartwarming part of the construction was the amount of volunteers laboring and those who raised money, from one dollar to several hundreds of dollars. The Gazebo was really becoming a Village project. I must confess, as I saw this beautiful project go forward I at times became very emotional because it was so great. Our Village was pulling together and as Mayor I had helped make it happen. Tears welled in my eyes when

I saw a good friend, Julius "Gibby" Giorgi, recovering from an almost fatal stroke, sitting in a chair in the hot sun laying brick to show his way of doing something for his home town. With his right arm, damaged by the stroke, he would place a brick with the mortar in place to build the foundation. This was truly an act of love of a human being for his community. With this kind of dedication and love for one's community the Gazebo was built, and the reason why it looks so imposing is probably because so much love went into its construction. With this labor of love and many donations of materials, the Village of Port Chester was able to construct a $65,000 Gazebo at a cost of only $7,000.

The formal dedication of the Gazebo was on July 23, 1983. At the final August, 1983 concert I presented Certificates of Appreciation to all who had a part in building this beautiful structure. A bronze plaque is in place that lists those officials that backed the project. Today the Gazebo serves every event at Lyon Park. I performed the first wedding under the star shaped roof for Sergeant Mike Bassano. The Byram River Arts Festival, the Christmas, Halloween, and Port Chester Day events also use our Gazebo. It truly has become a very useable structure. As I sit for our annual Friday concerts and the lights go on automatically as our Port Chester Pops Band plays, the scene is so impressive and lovely. It becomes New England revisited. Maybe someday when I leave politics, maybe a Board of Trustees would name the Gazebo in my honor.

In June 1993, the Gazebo was named the "Mayor Peter Iasillo Gazebo."

GOLDIE SOLOMON

If there was ever a person who could give Anacin a headache, that person is Goldie Solomon. If there ever was a citizen whose mouth, whose contemptuous attitude got her into more verbal scraps, Goldie led the pack. A person who maybe, and I repeat maybe, loved her community too much and brought to Port Chester much recognition, even bad, because of her public statements. Her interruptions at public meetings, her constant irritation to public officials and citizens alike led her to being ejected from many meetings. Her remarks were often irrational; often giving comments at public hearings on subjects that were not being discussed made me laugh at most times, and others made me want to gag her.

I appointed her chairperson of both the tri-centennial and bicentennial commissions hoping that her energy, ideas, and love of country would somehow calm her down and do a good job. At the beginning she was fantastic, with very innovative programs, like the swearing in of new citizens in our courtroom, which affected me very emotionally. But with Goldie's planning, the County Clerk's office felt like lynching her because of the problems she presented to them. Her love of antiquity, of historical buildings, and artifacts of our community were commendable in thought, but her actions literally turned off many in the community.

During her presidency of the Historical Society, I guess more people dropped out because of Goldie. Her actions in regards to trying to enlist the community to boycott our first Port Chester Day Festival because we were selling beer bordered on the absurd. Her attempts at instigating the NAACP to take actions against the Village on our "Halloween in the Park" were unfortunate, insulting, and stupid. Her attempts at staging bicentennial band concerts were poorly planned and resulted in failures. But she continued to try to do her thing, oblivious to her reputation and character being considered laughable and ludicrous. I think, and this is only my opinion, that Goldie is a very lonely woman. This is based on the fact that there were many times I saw her at restaurants eating alone. People tended to shy away from her because it invariably ended in either a shouting match or loud, bellowing conversations.

But with all this foolishness, Goldie faithfully attended Village Board meeting, giving her opinions and advice, which really all citizens should do. She made meetings vibrant at times and made politicians at election time seek her support. I never sought her support and felt happier by my decision. Every community has a Goldie Solomon, the activist, the stubborn and irritating person. Do communities need them to keep elected officials on their toes? I do not think so. The continued pressure to have an agenda addressed and publicity from the media only damages the image and luster of a community.

In 1991 Goldie chose to run against me for Mayor. Her issues were idiotic and I beat her handily as I received 60% of the vote. The press recognizes her as a political gadfly who gets press and really only makes her community look foolish.

But deep down she is an emotional citizen who if became more subdued would be a definite asset to Port Chester.

HELEN MARSHALL

If there is one thing any public official needs, it is the devotion, love, and understanding of his constituency. The one constituent who fervently sung my praises and had a degree of loyalty that any person, public official or otherwise, would cherish was Helen Rozmus Marshall. Only five feet tall, not really vivacious, thin, and with an affection for wearing a "Vince Lombardi" type winter cap even in the summertime, Helen had a temper. She could use phrases that included words not heard in churches and a voice that would drive birds out of trees. She would most times wear t-shirts supplied to her by Village staff people or politicians. It was not surprising to see her wearing six to eight t-shirts at one time. With her white sneakers and wool stocking, she presented a picture that most people perceived as comical or that of a bag woman. But make a statement about Mayor Iasillo and she would let go with a few choice words and put her 90 pounds into a left hook to the jaw. Many friends counseled me against her friendship for the fear that it would embarrass me, but how could I not love this devoted, friendly bundle of dynamite? One had only to look in her eyes to see the kindness she possessed. At any public function she would shriek out loud, "Pete Iasillo, the greatest Mayor in the world." With me at 6'3, 300 pounds, hugging this tiny, good friend, we surely presented a comical picture.

In March 1987 after a really difficult mayoral campaign, my dear wife

Gloria and I were preparing to go to the restaurant to listen for the final election returns. I told Gloria that win or lose I wanted her next to me when the returns were announced. As there would be Cable TV coverage, I especially wanted her next to me. Well, at the restaurant the returns came in and I was the victor for a fourth term. I bounded up to the stage to accept the cheers and applause. Amid all the yelling and jubilation, I announced that the person who should be with me was my beautiful, loving, and faithful wife Gloria. I yelled, "Gloria, come up here with me." Gloria, slightly handicapped, forced to use a cane, and not moving too swiftly, inched toward the stage. But who jumped up on the stage and proceeds to hug and try to kiss me but Helen Marshall! What a scene. I had to explain quickly to the TV cameras that Helen was not my wife.

Amid this confusion and laughing, Helen kept hugging me. The result was a page one-color photo of Helen and I in 50,000 copies of the Gannett newspapers and the Greenwich Times. I will never forget that evening. God bless Helen Marshall, a true loyal and good friend.

MARRIAGES

One of the nicest and happiest tasks that a Mayor of a Village performs is uniting two persons in marriage. Officiating at marriages has provided me with some of the happiest and funniest moments in my life as Mayor. When I first started to perform these marriages, my lovely wife, Gloria, questioned me as to the legality of the ceremony. My good friend, Deacon Jack Munnick, questioned me as to whether or not I was, by performing these marriages, committing a sin as interpreted by Roman Catholic religion. In both cases, I assured my wife and Deacon Jack that what I was doing was both legal and not sinful. As I look back on these marriages, some have left a lasting impression that lifted my spirits and provided real laughs. You must understand that I kept the ceremony as solemn as possible. However, there were some incidents that literally cracked me up, that made the reading of the ceremony almost impossible.

First of all, you must remember my clerk, Fritz Falanka, saw something comical in some of the couples and immediately told me, which cracked us up before I started. Then when the couple entered my office and I saw up front what he was referring to; I had all I could do from bursting out in laughter.

One particular marriage dealt with an extremely pretty girl, whose origin was from Colombia, South America. She was really a knockout. Dressed in a dark blue suit with a plunging neckline, she was really a vision to behold. Her jet-black hair was done up very fashionably. In effect, everything was perfect. As I read through the ceremony, Fritz Falanka and my secretary at the time, Marie Fallanca, were grinning, making faces and making it almost impossible to conclude the ceremony without laughing out loud. As I ended the ceremony, declaring the couple husband and wife, Marie and Fritz pointed to the bride's legs. As I looked I was astonished for her legs had hair all over them. It looked as if she grew Brillo. When they left my office, Marie fell to her knees, tears streaming down her cheeks laughing out loud at what she saw. Fritz was also laughing uproariously and I have to admit, I also had tears in my eyes. We wondered how could this vision, this bride so beautiful, never shave her legs?

We later found out that this was the custom of her country and was considered very feminine to have your legs engulfed in hair. It certainly was a sight I won't ever forget.

Then there was a young girl about to be married who asked to go to the ladies room before the service. She had black jeans on when she entered the ladies room, and changed into white jeans for the ceremony. Immediately after the ceremony, she then changed into her black jeans. I often wondered if her wearing white jeans were her way of proclaiming that she was a virgin. And speaking of a virgin, at one wedding when I instructed a witness or witnesses to sign the wedding license, one witness signed, and her first name was "Virgin Mary." I, jokingly, after seeing her signature said to her, "Hey, I've been praying to you for such a long time, it is a pleasure to meet you." She, not knowing of my sense of humor replied, "Oh, I no her, I no who you think I am, I just have the same name."

One wedding I will absolutely never forget. It was a Saturday morning outside our old Village Hall on Willett Avenue. About 10:00 a.m. I heard outside the Mayor's office window, which was right on sidewalk level, the sound of motorcycles. As they continually revved up their bikes, I peered out the Venetian blinds and I saw about nine bikers attired in ragged jeans, sleeveless shirts, tattoos on their arms, and I hoped they were not the group I had to marry. Well in a few seconds I heard the bang-bang at the front door. As I came to the door, a burly fellow about 6' 4" tall, with long hair, beard and hefty arms filled with tattoos, asked thunderously if I was the Mayor. When I replied that I was, he then stated that they were here to get his friends married. As they all entered my office, I thought to myself, "Oh boy, am I in a jam." I can tell you I was a little frightened. I kept thinking of the Marlon Brando film about bikers and their meanness. Well, I started the ceremony. The big, burly biker was the best man. The groom was a short fellow dressed in a three-piece suit, but the tattoos went up his neck past the white collar of his shirt, and very visible. The bride was an attractive young woman and had on a dress with a plunging neckline and thin straps. I started to read the ceremony and half way through the reading I noticed that she had a rose tattooed over her left breast.

I don't know what possessed me at the time, but I stopped reading and said to her, "The tattoo, it's very nice." She said, "thank you" and I finished the ceremony. After the bride and groom kissed, I noticed the groom and best man, the burly giant; both had tears in their eyes. As they left I said to myself, "Boy, you sure can't figure out people."

Another comical wedding involved the groom being married for the second time. After we went through the initial pleasantries and the signing of the license by the witnesses, the groom pulls out a paper from his jacket and informs me that it is a wedding contract for his bride to sign and if I would be a witness. Well, let me tell you, that's when the fun began. The bride, first of all, was stunned by the fact that she knew nothing of a contract, and let her husband-to-be know in no uncertain terms that she was not happy about seeing or hearing of the contract for the first time. An argument proceeded between the prospective bride and groom. I was asked to intervene, to mediate the contract, which I flatly refused. The result of the argument was that they left, not married, still arguing, and their witnesses apologizing to me. I often wonder if they finally got married, as they never came back to the Mayor's office.

Then there were the times a marriage was performed where the bride-to-be was pregnant. I would make a joke as I looked at the bride-to-be's large stomach, with child, and say that her large stomach would go down after the baby was born, but that the Mayor's rather portly body, with his large stomach, would remain. This seemed to ease them, as some of the brides were a little embarrassed by their pregnancy. One bride-to-be, a really large young woman, was 8 1/2 months pregnant. I instructed her to sit on the couch as I performed the ceremony and please don't sneeze or cough. I really felt that she was ready to give birth at any minute and any strong sneeze or cough would have the baby enter the world. I found out later that three days later she did indeed have a baby boy.

Probably the funniest wedding concerned a bride and groom from White Plains who wanted to be married in Port Chester. It was obvious from the start that the groom wore a rug, a wig, and not a very good one.

It was slightly off center as it sat on his head. It was a very funny sight. After introductions I asked for the wedding license.

Search as he would in his suit and the bride's pocketbook they didn't have the license. By now the sweat was dripping from under his wig. He said that it might be in his auto. He searched and searched. The result; no license. The sweat was really dripping from under his wig and it was starting to move all the more around his bald head. I suggested he go to White Plains to get a copy of the license. He got in his car and sped off to White Plains and got back in 30 -35 minutes with a copy of the license. He was sweating really heavily now and the wig had spun around on his head at least 90 degrees. We were now ready to start the ceremony. However, he had no witness. It meant I had to search outdoors for a witness. Fortunately, my friend "Ozzie" Zumpano came by and reluctantly agreed to be witness. His reluctance was based on his clothes. He had a sleeveless shirt and a pair of Bermuda shorts, the ends being frayed with grease stains over the front. Well, finally after an hour or so I performed the marriage. Too bad we didn't have a photographer. What a sight. "Ozzie," the best man, nattily attired in his beat up shorts and the groom, sweating profusely with the wig on his head, had spun around and was now cocked off to one side. What a picture it would have been.

There was also a wedding I performed between a white male and a black woman. He was not only extremely nervous but also seemed very much in love. The bride seemed very edgy and annoyed with the groom. After the conclusion of the marriage, I normally ask them to kiss. Her reply was, "Do I have to?" I replied, "No." The husband made a move to kiss her; she turned away and he ended up kissing her hair, which stuck to his lips. The hair then became separated because it was a wig. That wasn't bad enough. Three months later, the husband visited me and said his bride had vanished and he wanted our Police Department to locate her. I referred him to the D.A.'s office. I later found out that she left him. The reason? He turned out to be a wimp and she was tired of belting him almost every day. My own opinion was that the man was a Looney-tune ... not a very stable person.

I also found out with rather large wedding parties, that people have a tendency to throw rice at the end of the ceremony. I have found rice after these particular ceremonies stuck in the TV set, in books, between papers on my desk, behind the couches, on bookshelves, etc.   Also, there have been numerous occasions when the party breaks open a bottle of champagne and it usually ends up all over the rug or the furniture. Another wedding I performed outdoors, in the backyard of the bride's mother's home, on a real sunny day, resulted in the bride's mother and the groom being stung by bees.

But there have also been really nice weddings. One particularly nice wedding was when I married a Police Sergeant, Mike Bisano, in Lyon Park in our Gazebo. This was the first wedding ever performed in our Gazebo. I've married children whose parents were close friends, and attended these weddings, and have known parents who didn't know of the weddings because the children wanted it kept a secret.

I've married real young people. I remember a pregnant sixteen-year-old girl, whose grandparents I knew personally, and sad at their predicament. Seniors, in their late 70's I've married. One I distinctly remember marrying and the groom sadly passed away three weeks later. Many of those I marry I often see and they lovingly point out their children and ask, "Do you remember me Mayor? You married us. This is our new baby." Sometimes I remember them, most times I do not. Being Mayor you are presented with many problems, many arguments, and many decisions to make. One thing is certain, marrying a couple and seeing them leave the office with a smile and the look of love in their eyes makes all the other problems seem trivial.

MICHAEL MENDICINO

When I entered politics in 1970, I was a real novice and an amateur. It didn't take me to long to realize that in both the Republican and Democrat parties there were workers, those leaders who toiled "in the trenches" getting out the vote for their party and their candidates. There were also the "phonies" that talked a good game but never delivered the votes. I remember in the 1970's the Republicans had hard leaders and workers such as Frank Zumpano, Joe Guglielmo (Williams) and Sid Greenberg.

There was one leader in the Democrat party that the Republicans continually talked about. The person who really could get out their vote in the Washington Park section of Port Chester was Mike "West" Mendicino.

Mike Mendicino was always the talk at Republican gatherings. In those 1970's, politics was ruthless. When your party was in the majority, you got all the good jobs. If you worked for the Village and were registered with the minority party, after an election you stood a good chance to be transferred from a supervisory position to just a laborer position. In those 1970's, elections were not political campaigns; they were wars. To the victor belonged the spoils. People like Mike Mendicino knew of this practice but didn't complain or cry baby this fact. They worked to get their guys in, no matter what the consequences might be.

I remember after our great Republican victory in 1970 there was a meeting of about 8 Republican leaders and elected officials. The reason for the meeting, what changes in jobs would there be? To my shock and surprise, the first change proposed would be the transfer of my good friend and neighbor Tony Scinto, a Democrat, from Assistant Foreman to a Laborer. I remember objecting violently to this action but I was told that this was the way the game was played. I was stunned. What to do? With no help or advice from anyone, I caved in and Tony Scinto was transferred. For several years Tony and his lovely wife Jennie ignored and snubbed Gloria and I. I couldn't blame them. This horrible practice of politics was not what I had ever thought it was. I determined from that point on that I would operate differently. Because of this I upset many Republicans. There was one worker the Republicans wanted to get. It was Mike Mendicino.

The Republicans were not successful. Mike was protected in his Village job. The Republicans also attempted to eliminate Mike from his job as a Bingo inspector but Mike thwarted this attempt. His war veteran status saved him, much to the dissatisfaction of the Republicans. Mike Mendicino was a dynamic and forceful person who worked, managed, and organized many election campaigns that saw Democrats rise to great heights. He was not disliked but actually hated by many politicians. It was during the McCrory administration in 1978-1980 that Mike and I became better friends.

Mike had been grand fathered from the Village Signs and Lines Department to the position of Court Clerk. Republicans complained of this move because they were really irked that they never thought of making this move with a Republican getting the job. A strong bond existed between Trustee Mike Pierro and Mike Mendicino. Trustee Pierro recognized the great help Mike gave him in his successful campaign and tried to make improvements in Mendicino's job. However, somehow Mayor McCrory seemingly rebuffed the suggestions to change Mike's job. In my own mind, I felt that what Mike was seeking was not overly ambitious. When the opportunity came, I supported Trustee Pierro's proposal. My action resulted in Mike and I becoming better friends. When I ran for Mayor in 1980 and won by only 24 votes, the talk around the political circles was that Mike really didn't knock himself out for Mayor McCrory and as a result, I won. Is this true? I don't know. But in the years that followed, Mike and I became closer friends.

Even some Republicans took a mellower attitude towards Mike. Mike had considered retiring in 1986 and requested one more year from the Republicans to stay on his job. We saw no need to force him out. However, during that time the Albany legislature passed a bill that stated age would not be a reason for retiring an employee. As a result, Mike stayed on until 1991. One fact should be brought out, there were many justices who served the Village who questioned Mike's competency as Court Clerk and requested that I relieve Mike from his position for this reason.

My answer to these judges was, "Put it in writing if you feel he is incompetent." Every one of the judges backed off. They expected me to be the bad guy. I refused because I remembered Tony Scinto in 1970 and was determined to refuse the practice of politically ruining the life of any employee as long as I was Mayor.

At Mike's retirement dinner he personally came to me and thanked me for my help in his years as a Court Clerk. This affirmation by Mike touched me very much. He and his wife Jean were real good, close friends.

MICHAEL D. RITCHIE

The year 1992, at budget time in Port Chester, proved to be a momentous time in the Village's history. In the short period of weeks, the Village lost all of its professionals due to a group I called the "Fallible Five," Trustees Gianfrancesco, Terenzi, Colangelo, McCrory, and DiRoberto. The start of another type of recession bloomed in Port Chester. The termination of Mike Ritchie finally happened. For years I kept together a coalition of Trustees that effectively stopped Mike's termination, but in 1992 when Terenzi and Gianfrancesco clasped hands along with the two Democrats, McCrory and DiRoberto, and God only knows why Colangelo jumped in, Mike Ritchie was done in. He was terminated, fired. The reasons given in the media by them for firing Ritchie was that Mike didn't fit into the Board's long-range plans. They never fully explained the long-range plans.

To my way of thinking, their real reason for going along with the "Fallible Five," was that a political survey by the Republicans was done before the 1992 Trustee election and Mike Ritchie's name was inserted in the survey. Why it was inserted I never found out. Mike got a large, unfavorable rating. As a result, maybe they thought that was proof enough to get rid of Ritchie or possibly they thought it could improve their own favorable rating. The thinking on their part was lacking reason or common sense. One gave his reason to the media for firing Ritchie was that "he got too cozy with the

Mayor." I guess he felt I should always be in confrontation or in opposition with the Manager. That thinking was surely irrational to say the least. My reasoning was that this was a way to destroy the good business relationship between the Manager and the Mayor. It was not good business sense, just a personal vendetta.

Mike Ritchie had stayed on as Manager for almost 15 years. His personal relationship with me for his last 12 years was very cordial. His cooperation with my ideas and seeing that they were carried out gave our Village much success, good media coverage, and several awards from New York State, Westchester County, and the Federal Government.

But it wasn't always that cordiality that existed at the beginning of my first term as Mayor.

Mike had operated almost two years as Manager under Mayor McCrory as both Manager and Chief Executive Officer. His powers were limitless. As a Trustee, I came into conflicts with Mike on numerous occasions and the bitterness between us was known to many. Mike wielded his power without, it seemed, any care or concern for our citizens or employees. The position of appointing Niels Hansen as the Superintendent of Public Works really brought us on a collision course. I was against it and felt that Mike played games with Hansen's resume that really brought us to grips. The result of the attempt to put Niels Hansen as our Superintendent of Public Works fizzled out due to a lawsuit brought forward by Sanitation Foreman "Faust" Summa.

It was probably this incident that made me most cognizant of the fact that the law regarding the Village Manager should be revised.

Naturally, when I suggested it and THE DAILY ITEM got wind of it, they immediately pounced on me. I took the blows from them knowing that they were wrong and that they misinterpreted what I was stating. I formed a committee consisting of Deputy Mayor Ray Hellman, ZBA Chairman Charlie Volker, businessman Paul Brezowsky, Democratic Party Chairman Tony Meloni, and Vice Chairman of the Democratic Party Lou Passarelli. The Village Corporation Counsel Sam Lerner also served as legal counsel. It was a bipartisan committee with the intelligence to grasp what I wanted to see accomplished. The seven-year law needed to be revised and I had a perfect committee to see it through completion. The committee, after six months, made their recommendations. The changes were adopted and just as I had predicted, the revised Manager law was much better than the original law and the relationship between Mike Ritchie and I improved.

Those early years, 1981 through 1987, were days of excitement and great accomplishments for our Village. Mike Ritchie and I worked with a wonderful understanding of what Port Chester needed, and who had to be contacted to move projects along. These years were probably the most fulfilling and happiest times I had as Mayor. When Tom Farrell came on board we really formed a "trinity." We met, had creative sessions, fashioned new projects, and made Port Chester come alive. These were times I will never forget. Unfortunately, these gratifying years came to an end with the termination of Mike Ritchie. Mike Ritchie was highly respected by his peers and while many residents of Port Chester were exhilarated by his firing, I felt his termination was uncalled for and merely a way of embarrassing the Mayor. It was ironic that an editorial in THE DAILY ITEM also agreed with my reasoning.

MID-EAST, FBI, STING OPERATIONS

I often wondered if many of our Port Chester residents ever knew that Port Chester had been the center of two sting operations. I say two because I was involved in two of them. For all I know, there may have been more. What is a sting operation?

When prosecutors and FBI agents set up public officials to commit illegal acts and then pounce on them and prosecute them with fines, imprisonment, or both, that is a sting operation.

The first sting operation occurred in the late 1970's. The first Village Manager of Port Chester, Pete Pakey, was hired by the Village Board. Although a review committee of private citizens endorsed his employment and praised his past record and employment, those in Village government, after several months, could see that he was far from being the best-qualified person for the post of Village Manager. Probably because of his deficiencies, he hired an FBI agent, Charlie Carpenter, in our Building Department. We, in government, did not know of this. Pakey obviously thought that by doing this he might come up with information that would enhance his ability to be a successful administrator. Since Port Chester was a highly political community, Pakey probably felt that the Building Inspectors, most especially Willie "Cheen" Santora and Joseph Suppa Sr., were on the take, making illegal deals that would garner them extra money. The FBI agent worked undercover for some time.

The result? There were no deals being made by any Building Inspectors and also that I had no ties to any illegal deals. I was lumped into the investigation because I had served, before the Village Manager Law was enacted, as the Finance Commissioner of the Village and had the responsibility over the Building Department. I often felt that my being regularly written up in the newspapers as an active Village official made me well known and the perfect public official on which to try a sting operation.

The second sting operation happened in 1988. After my brothers and I sold our business in 1986, I was out of work for several months. I was offered a position with Byram Concrete by the Luiso brothers. They felt my knowledge of private investors and entrepreneurs in my years as Mayor could enhance their position in the construction business. It was also felt that my position as Mayor would open the doors to large corporations and their CEO's. They were right. That is just what happened. Later on when the construction industry waned, Ron Luiso, because of business difficulties, had to lay me off. This reaction affected me and was determined by my doctor as one reason for my September heart attack. That's another story.

I had just concluded a rather traumatic inquiry by our Ethics Committee. I had suspected for some time that the FBI was possibly tapping my phones. I guess they felt that there was something they could hang on me.

My reputation as a Mayor in Westchester County was well known. My popularity with my peers was fantastic. I was well respected and possibly because of my continuous tenure in office, even after all the bad publicity I had received from the media, to get me would have been a prize for the FBI. As a result I continually found myself checking my rearview mirror to see if I was being followed. Strange clicks on my phones made my wife and I very suspect, and I even had to be careful of my funny sense of humor, which I was known for, as a remark might have been taken out of context and used against me.

In 1988, a police sergeant approached me with an idea for both of us to make a great deal of money. Due to my knowledge and acquaintanceship with many developers through my position as Mayor and as the Marketing Director of Byram Concrete, I would be aware of which developers were in a position to seek financing to develop new properties or to continue projects they had in the works. The idea was simple. I would approach these developers, question if they were seeking new financing or re-financing and refer them to an individual who would meet with them and offer financing at extremely suitable interest rates.

I instantly knew of one such developer who would be ideal for this rather simple way of getting loans. You must understand that we were talking big bucks, millions, and the finder's fee to me would have been tremendous.

The individual who would make the contact with the developer was an attorney from Rye Brook, New York. The police sergeant arranged a dinner meeting in which the three of us would outline our tasks. At this dinner meeting, I learned that the money would come from the Mid-East (Iraq, Saudi Arabia, and Kuwait) shahs with a bundle of oil money to invest. I was to find those who needed this money and arrange a meeting with the attorney and he would see to it that a deal would be consummated. The thought of the money I could make was mind boggling, and clouded my vision as to what I was getting myself into. I did, however, tell them that I would not involve myself with any projects slated for Port Chester.

Everything was set. I approached the developer I knew of, from Armonk, a good friend, and he was immediately agreeable. He had two projects that needed financing, and this was a great and easy way to get this financing. He met with the attorney and after some weeks I was told that although the developer was perfect for the loan the only thing that killed the deal was that the developer was only seeking $10-12 million dollars which was not enough to satisfy the lenders. They were talking of deals of a minimum of $40-50 million dollars.

This should have made me suspect, but the thought of the dollars I could make in finders fee again clouded my senses. So, I continued my search for developers in need of big bucks.

Then, approximately one month after the deal with the Armonk developer was killed, I received a call from a good, dear friend, Bill Cassin. The call was at about 7:30 in the evening. I remember we were celebrating the birthday of a member of my family and Bill asked if I could meet with him that evening. I replied in the affirmative and in about ten minutes I heard his horn tooting. I invited him in but he insisted I sit in his car. I did and Bill started to go around the block. Oh, I forgot to mention that Bill Cassin was a former FBI agent. As we rode, he inquired if I had been approached by anyone to work with or assist in trying to loan money to developers. I answered in the affirmative and outlined to him how I was involved and what the plans were. When I finished, Bill then told me to keep away from this as it was a sting operation by the FBI and I was being set up. He was amazed that the idea of Mid-East money was again being used in this sting by the FBI.

I listened intently and as the pieces came together, regarding the sergeant, the attorney, the Mid-East shahs, etc.; indeed I then realized I was being set up.

In the weeks that followed, I never returned any phone calls from the sergeant. He appeared one Saturday morning at my home and asked me if he could speak with me. I let him in and he then described another facet of his plan to get me money. He stated that they, the attorney and the shahs, realized that the only way I could really line up developers was if I had an office. It would in actuality be a dummy office and they were ready to pay me an upfront fee of $75,000 to man this dummy office a few hours a week and the compensation of $75,000 was a gift to compensate me for all I had tried to do so far. Although I was steaming inside and wanted to blurt out what I knew, I just calmly replied that I did not want to be involved. That ended it for me and the plan to make me rich.

I found out later that the police sergeant was in debt to the IRS for back taxes. His reward to set me up was that the Feds would forgive him for his taxes. The friend who really helped me, Bill Cassin, has since died. I will never forget his helping me. I remember him many times in my days as I travel and I pray for his soul. I don't know what the conclusion would have been if he hadn't warned me. I now carefully think out any statement that I make and any phone call I make or receive.

PORT CHESTER YACHT CLUB

The question that has been asked many times, "How did the Village ever come up with a 20-year lease for the Port Chester Yacht Club with such a small amount of rental at $1,800 a year?" I guess that has baffled many Village residents for the past two decades. Well, now it can be told. It will shock some, it will upset some people to reveal what happened, but the time is appropriate to disclose how it came about. The time was before the 1974 mayoral election. Joe Dzaluk, after being Mayor from 1970 to 1972, decided not to run for re-election in 1972. Dom Bambace, who won the 1972 election for Mayor, was now set to run as incumbent in 1974. His opponent was Joe Dzaluk who decided to return to the political wars. The campaign promised to be very interesting as Dom Bambace with his two running mates for Village Trustee seats, were two incumbents and powerful vote getters, Phil Fidelibus and Carl Scmehl. Joe Dzaluk's two running mates for Trustee were two new faces, Joe Carlucci and Bill Davidson. One thing must be said for Joe Dzaluk is that he left no stone unturned in seeking victory. He reasoned a block of votes that he felt would be ready to confer with the Yacht Club, whom we heard was turned down by Dom Bambace for what reason I didn't know. Joe, along with Dan LaDore and myself, were to have a special meeting with Yacht Club members to discuss plans mutually acceptable to both parties.

We should have realized that their conferring with Dom Bambace first was reason enough to believe that they felt Dom would win the election and not Joe.

The night we met was in the cellar of a Yacht Club member on Fox Island Road. There was a string of incandescent lights hanging from the ceiling as we met, not even florescent lights. It was a funny, eerie scene. You would think it was the meeting of a secret society. I had all to do to keep from laughing out loud at the secretiveness and foolishness of the meeting place. The conversation dealt with the Yacht Club throwing their support behind Joe Dzaluk and the Republican ticket in the upcoming election for a lease on the property currently used by the Yacht Club. It should be noted that Joe Carlucci and Bill Davidson were not aware of the meeting. Good thing or the whole meeting would have been concluded real quickly, without an agreement.

As one looks back at this meeting and the agreement to help the Yacht Club, one should realize that the property in question backed up to our local landfill site (dump), there were industrial buildings, a foul smelling sewage disposal plant and our Village incinerator all in close proximity to the Yacht Club. No one really concerned themselves with the Yacht Club and the property. No one could even conceive that approximately ten years later, the property would be valuable beyond our wildest dreams. In hindsight the lease was a bad deal, but in 1974 it seemed to us to be a good deal. We were agreeing to lease a piece of land that no one cared about and no one disputed, for signing the contract to the long term lease was public knowledge. It was not secretive. Joe Dzaluk and the Republicans won the election. After years later in analyzing this election I now believe Joe Dzaluk and his team won because they worked harder than their opponents. It definitely was not the Yacht Club's support that did the job. There were those in the Republican Party, who by the way were Yacht Club members, who for years and years felt the Yacht Club was the force that won the 1974 campaign. I refute those assumptions and point to my own re-election victories, without the Yacht Club's endorsement or blessings, as an indicator that the Yacht Club never controlled votes and elections.

The real turmoil and problems associated with the Yacht Club boiled over in 1984 when the Village realized, through extensive interest by developers in waterfront properties, that they, now indeed in a lease agreement with the Yacht Club, had to recapture the property in question. There was too much at stake and the Village's interests, long term, meant canceling the lease. That's when the real trouble started.

The Village Board decided at the time we should start negotiations with the Yacht Club to seek a method to cancel the lease and hear the Yacht Club's proposal for what they required to cancel the lease. I, along with Corporation

Counsel Sam Lerner, and Village Trustee John Branca, were selected to be the negotiating team for the Village. From the start these turned out to be the wrong choices. Sam Lerner was too straightforward and at times abrasive, and John Branca, as it was obvious from the first meeting, was linked too emotionally and personally with the Yacht Club. From the opening gun, I could see the meetings would go nowhere and it was clear that the Village and the Yacht Club were on a collision course. We (the Village) declared the lease illegal and void citing a December 27, 1974 letter from the New York State Attorney General's office stating such.

In a letter dated September 12, 1984, from Sam Lerner to the Yacht Club's attorney, (which I have every reason to believe no one knows of), Lerner cited what would or could be done at the lease cancellation such as reimbursing the Yacht Club for improvements made by them, that the Village Board would provide for public access and use of the waterfront for the Club and the entire community. We also declared the Club to be a private club and not a "public facility." We were going nowhere in our meetings. Great trouble was on its way. Lawsuits were now going to fly back and forth. The Village and the Yacht Club were going to war. How long it would last we did not know nor could we predict. What the consequences would be, the viciousness of the confrontations between the Village and the Yacht Club for years to come loomed greatly over the horizon. Friendships would be broken, families would feud, the fallout would be immense.

On July 25, 1985, the New York Supreme Court ruled the Yacht Club lease invalid and eviction could proceed if the Village wanted to. On an appeal by the Yacht Club to the U.S. District Court on July 30, 1985, the appeal was dismissed. But as the Yacht Club attorney predicted, "This dismissal is by no means the end of the story. It's the beginning of the story." Then at a really heated August 6, 1985 Board meeting, the Village Board voted 6-1 to seek plans for the Fox Island 18.5 acres (including the Yacht Club leased land). It was evident at that meeting that the Yacht Club issue was really heating up.

After that heated meeting, an editorial writer for THE DAILY ITEM, William Bookman, wrote a slanted, pro-Yacht column, disparaging the Village's attempts at development at the Fox Island site. I answered him in a "Letter to the Editor" contending his views were biased and his story contained many inaccuracies. Needless to say, THE DAILY ITEM again had another reason to put me on their hate list.

In October 1985, the Appellate Division of the State Supreme Court delayed the eviction of the Yacht Club until January 1986. By this time lawsuits were flying consistently. The Yacht Club's treasury estimated at $90,000 was now being tapped with great severity. Then in May 1986, the three-judge panel of the Appellate Term of the State Supreme Court ruled that Rye Town Judge Reuben Sirlin's decision that the Yacht Club vacate the leased land was valid. Would this end the case? Hell no! Another appeal was filed by the Yacht Club. Now the Club hired a high priced New York City law firm and their treasury would now suffer even more. A year later, in October 1986, a four-judge panel of the State Supreme Court now reversed the three-judge panel's decision and declared the Yacht Club lease valid. The waters being stirred even more by this new development. It was also reported that the Yacht Club was also now linking arms with dissident merchants to stop or curtail the Robert Martin Downtown Development. In February 1987, the Village Board unanimously, finally, picked a developer for the Fox Island site, James Harvie and Partners of White Plains.

At this time another mayoral election came forward. Once again I was victorious, by a comfortable margin, over a Village Trustee, Nick Fusco, a 16-year veteran on the Village Board. In July 1987, a four-judge Appellate Division panel now ruled that the Village and the Yacht Club go to trial to see if the Yacht Club's use of the leased property was public or private. Things stayed pretty quiet until May 1988, when the New York based attorneys for the Yacht Club, at an open meeting, criticized the Village's environmental report on our waterfront revitalization plan. The attorney's speech drew much applause from Yacht Club members in attendance, but the speech was like "firing a gun filled with blanks," all noise, no substance.

Then, in late July 1988, the Village Board authorized the Mayor to sign an agreement with James Harvie and Partners that would start the process to develop the Fox Island site, including the Yacht Club property. More arguments came from the Yacht Club attorney, which meant that the Yacht Club's treasury was being further depleted. It was also at this time the State Legislature, through our assemblyman Ron Tocci, was drafting a bill to allow the lifting of certain restrictions on waterfront property. In August 1988, the contract between the Village and James Harvie was officially signed.

The spring 1989 mayoralty election came about. I was pitted against Trustee Vincent Sapione, an ardent Yacht Club member and the individual who started the Landmark investigation. The campaign was not as dirty as I thought it would be. Once again with the Yacht Club endorsing Sapione, I still handily beat Sapione for my fifth term. In May, 1989, the EPA decided to test the property on the 18.5 acre site, and also the DEC. In the spring of 1990, the Republicans again won their election and the task of getting the bill through the New York State Legislature was commenced. In May 1990, the Board authorized the submission of a Home Rule Request to move the bill forward. In April 1990, a meeting was held between three Yacht Club members and the Mayor and Trustees Branca and Gianfrancesco. The result was that we impressed upon the Yacht Club members what was already known to all regarding the Harvie Plan. We left the meeting thinking that we had accomplished a start to further negotiations. No such way. We were still at a point of head knocking. However, in June 1990, the Yacht Club did now feel the time was right to start negotiations.

Conclusion: I felt nothing would ever happen to peacefully end what had gone on since the first confrontation in 1984.

Maybe in 1994 when the lease ends the Yacht Club will realize what we planned to do at the waterfront would benefit them more than what they have now. Through bad advice, untruthful statements by the Club's hierarchy, a boating club turned political, they spent thousands of dollars foolishly and created hatreds that will endure for many years.

SAM LERNER

As one reads these memoirs, it is obvious that I put great importance on the word loyalty. Any elected official needs it to survive. Politics is a dirty game in which today's friends can overnight become enemies. It is a game where the weak struggle and waffle back and forth on issues that sometimes are made by weak individuals whose decisions are based on not what is best for all but rather on who yells and screams the loudest. After the untimely death of my good friend and Corporation Counsel Ed Saltzman, I needed a person for this post that could give me the backing, the counseling, and loyalty that I needed if the plans I had in mind for Port Chester would succeed. Where Ed Saltzman was a gentle, calm, and peaceful individual, the person I chose was at most times the complete opposite. I asked a registered Democrat, a former classmate at Port Chester High School, Sam Lerner, to serve as my Corporation Counsel.

Sam and I after many years out of school were still very close friends. There was no question in my mind that Sam could handle the job as Corporation Counsel. He served with some distinction as a Rye Town Councilman in the administration of "Chappie" Posillipo. Because of Sam's honesty and conformity to the government and legal ethics, at times he gave "Chappie" problems. He was not a member of the round table, those politicians who sat for lunch at the Sawpit Restaurant on Saturdays with "Chappie" and his friends. The two words that really described Sam were honest and outspoken. Convincing my Republican majority on Sam's appointment was somewhat difficult, since he was a registered Democrat. However, I had proved to the Republican Party for over two years that being in bed with any particular party regular does not guarantee good appointments.

I suggested that registered Democrats could prove to be in the best interests of the Republican Party and most of all the Village of Port Chester. My appointments of Democrats in my first two years as Mayor proved this. They included Nick Fusco, Deputy Mayor; Roland Berlingo, Village Justice; Fritz Falanka, Village Clerk; Lou Passarelli, Planning Commission; and Frank Torascio, Zoning Board of Appeals.

The thing that really helped in this appointment was Sam's great track record as Chairman of the Industrial Development Agency, (IDA). When Sam took over as Chairman of the IDA, it had been floundering and didn't involve itself in the forward movement of Port Chester. Sam had great visions for Port Chester, he was now a resident of the Village of Rye Brook, and I guess the two of us together really started the dynamism that was needed to have Port Chester move ahead. His bluntness presented me with problems, as several Republican Board members were irritated that I would recommend a Democrat for a position of such sensitivity as Corporation Counsel; but they were naive and couldn't stand to hear the truth. Sam Lerner, when making remarks to the Board of Trustees, let it all hang out. The niceties that the late Ed Saltzman brought to Village government were clearly a memory when it came to Sam Lerner.

I guess the three most important matters that Sam involved himself in as Corporation Counsel, up to 1986, were the Yacht Club lease, the Harbor Development, and the Downtown Marina Development. The Yacht Club, other than the landmark ethics investigation, presented me with my biggest problem of my administration. It was a problem I cover solely in another chapter, a problem that brought bitterness, threats to my family, a split of several Republican Trustees, and an issue in every political campaign for over six years. It really started when Sam, John Branca, and I were chosen to confer with the Yacht Club to come up with a solution to either cancel their lease that they had with the Village or seek a peaceful solution, if possible, regarding the Yacht Club remaining at the site. From the very start of these negotiations, it was obvious that we were headed on a collision course. Sam's sometimes bluntness and terse remarks did nothing to make the negotiations any easier. When you add to this that the Yacht Club believed they had the Village over a barrel, and the stubbornness of the Yacht Club's negotiators, you had a clear-cut recipe for arguments and bitter disputes. Once the lawsuits came in rapid progression, the case was turned over to attorneys representing our insurance carriers.

While I agree, to this day, that Sam's opinions regarding the case were right, and legal, I guess in retrospect the question of Sam's demeanor and also that of the Yacht Club attorney proved to be a stumbling block to calm, composed discussions.

When in 1986 the Democrats gained control of the Village Board, Sam was not reappointed. His successor lasted about a year, followed by Ray Falcon. When the Republicans gained the majority in 1988, the appointment was to Willis Stephens. My conversation clearly showed that he was not concerned about returning as Corporation Counsel. He felt that a position as Assistant Corporation Counsel would be strictly in the field of legal advice on future developments such as the Robert Martin Development and the Harbor Development contract negotiations. In this arena Sam was well suited because of his years of experience as Chairman of the IDA. As special counsel Sam's expertise and knowledge helped immensely as these two projects moved forward. When it got to the point that advising on both these projects and trying to still maintain his law practice proved too much, the Robert Martin Development Project was turned over to a large New York City law firm. Maybe this was a blessing in disguise because Sam always had his doubts as to whether we were giving away the store on this project.

At this point Sam's legal advice was now strictly geared to assisting Tom Farrell at OPD on the Harvie Harbor Development Project. A slight strain in our personal relationship came in mid 1990, referring to Gary Gianfrancesco as covered in the Chapter "Young Turks I." I guess looking back on this matter, Sam in his own unique fashion figured that it was to my benefit to give in somewhat on the matter. I told Sam of my disappointed in his involvement in this matter because I felt the question in point was a political matter and to my way of thinking, Sam Lerner was probably the worst political analyst and advisor in the Rye Town area. In fact, I always told this to Sam. I still valued his friendship. His advice to me on the Landmark ethics case was right and I didn't take it, which probably could have saved me much aggravation and bad publicity. I sincerely believe he was always looking out for my behalf. We still had one great discussion, who was the better one at basketball. I knew I was, but my pal Sam would not give in.

He still contended pound for pound he had it all over me. His untimely death of cancer, after I retired as Mayor, left me once again with a great loss of a great friend.

SERAFINO GUIDO

"I pledge allegiance to the flag of the United States of America..." Sounds familiar, of course, it is our pledge to the symbol of our country, the Stars and Stripes, Old Glory, our Flag. There burst upon the scene in 1978 a retired sergeant from the Marine Corps, Serafino Guido, whose fanaticism to see the flag flown on every Village owned flagpole caused agitation that affected the administrations of both Mayor McCory and me. His emotional tirades at monthly Board meetings led newspapers to frequently report his feelings and describe him in terms of a real patriot, and the elected officials as not knowledgeable of the flag and not really caring for the flag and the U.S.A. He frequently accused officials of being traitors and this type of outburst from him precipitated many local, vocal arguments at Board meetings. He wrote letters to the President of the United States, the FBI the CIA, the Commandant of the Marine Corps, all voicing his opinion that the Port Chester officials were traitorous. His outbursts became so inflammatory at one particular meeting that Trustee John Connolly, a great Trustee and a real gentleman stated quite loudly to Serafino, "Mr. Guido, there is one good thing about having two earpieces; I can shut off people whose absurdities upset me." With that Mr. Connolly put his fingers to his ears and turned off his earpieces.

No matter how loud Serafino addressed the Trustee, Mr. Connolly merely smiled and gazed about the meeting room.

In 1979 I suggested and introduced a resolution that the Village erect a monument to those boys of Port Chester who died in the Vietnam War. At the time, anything associated with the Vietnam War was scorned, frowned upon, and just not thought to be worth the time and trouble. As Chairman of the Committee to erect this monument, when the day came to dedicate it on November 11, 1979, I had designated Sgt. Guido to raise the American flag for the first time up the flagpole. Sgt. Guido was so honored by the invitation that he planned to wear his dress green Marine uniform. It required him to lose weight to fit into the uniform, but he was determined and started to diet vigorously.

The day of the ceremony, sure enough, Sgt. Guido arrived in a taxi at the site of dedication. He exited the taxi clutching the Stars and Stripes which the night before he would not give up the American flag to one of our Highway Dept. personnel, and who he threatened bodily harm if he tried to take the flag. As he exited from the cab we noticed how straight and erect he stood and walked. He was the epitome of the "John Wayne" type, ramrod straight. As he stood there with a large cluster of ribbons denoting the medals and awards he had received as a Marine, it was only then that we learned he had fit into his uniform because he was wearing a corset. The Sergeant now lives in Arkansas with his daughter. While in Port Chester he had caused quite a stir, but he did write me a touching letter when he left Port Chester praising me for my efforts in trying to upgrade our Village. He had a point to make and he persisted in his quest of making the Village and their officials more aware of our flag and its importance in our lives.

THE DAILY ITEM

How does a daily newspaper whose whole structure was created to service a community with news and stories that were factual and carefully written change so dramatically to become one that is scorned and despised by its readers? Such was THE DAILY ITEM. Where the readers used to look to articles that were once informative and honest in it's reporting, they read a newspaper that had become almost vicious at times, using innuendo and crudeness to promote their stories with the intent to disgrace public officials. Rather than seek the truth or to hear two sides of a story, it was a paper that carried grudges against any official that would oppose them, knowing full well that they have the last word and will literally crush anyone who stands in their way.

This was a newspaper that had become a factory for yellow journalism, whose respect was once touted to the highest heavens by its readers. It was now not only despised and disrespected by public officials, but also by its readers who openly stated they bought the newspaper mainly for the obituary column, which the paper also screwed up.

I can remember an editor of a past DAILY ITEM, Ed Hughes, who in a professional and respectful way was an editor that did indeed report the news, gave all the facts, and did not reach the point of acting as a judge in matters affecting the Village. He left that to his readers. They, the readers, made the judgment after reading factual news stories, not stories slanted in such a way to embarrass or humiliate a public official or anyone involved in government. I remember when Louis "Chip" Weil took over as publisher of the Gannett chain and stated, "You have told us you want more and better news of your community. We are changing our newspapers to do just that." He also stated, "Readers want local news in their local newspapers, and we must deliver it in greater quantity and higher quality than ever before." While Mr. Weil's statements were high sounding and the column in which he wrote these high sounding words was titled, "A Rededication to Local News," it was just a smoke screen for the real motives of the Gannett chain. Those motives, most people perceived, were to insult and disgrace officials and intimidate them into following the newspaper's ideas.

Thank God there are still public officials who won't be coerced or dominated by the newspapers who use their own ideas of honesty and courage to continue their fight. While THE DAILY ITEM tried to fool the public into thinking they were performing a service that the reader looked to in order to to form an honest opinion, they were really trying to lead their readers by pandering to their prejudices and passions. If you looked it up in Webster's Dictionary you would find that this type of action is defined as demagoguery, and if you also consulted the Dictionary you would find that being "careless of rule and accuracy, especially in literary matters, exceeding the limits of propriety" is defined as being licentious.

THE DAILY ITEM and its editors should have searched their souls and their consciences to see if they were acting responsively or acting as demagogues whose actions or statements bordered on being licentious.

Clearly how can a newspaper report on local news when their staff writers leave the newspaper so often? If any business had a turnover in its employees as did THE DAILY ITEM, I would wonder if their business were really knowledgeable of the facts in any community. It would seem that just when the staff writer knows the community, its public officials, its employees, its citizens (including the sane ones, the nuts, the loudmouths, the publicity seekers, the crazies, etc.) they have the staff writer leave the newspaper.

From 1980 to August 1990, the following were involved as staff writers covering the Village of Port Chester: Doug Williams, Bob Libbey, Lisa Iervolino, Mike Meaney, Roger Cawley, Lesta Cordil, Scott Faubel, Joey Asher, Georgette Gouvei, John , Vivian Dennis, Donna Greene, Bill Hoffman, Vic Aiminsky, Marc Moran, Brenda Hettman, Sydney Stanton, Peggy Edersheim, Michael Slackman, K.J. White, Tom Anderson, Catherine Ryan, Sandra James, Albert Jiminez,, Denise DeStephen, Bill Dentzer, Arthur Kroeber, Joshua Peck, Victoria Harmon, Melissa Conti, Gail Gorman, Lawrence Hooper, Carol A. Hayes, Kathy Mickey, Jamie Shankman, Irene

Zutell, Hayley Gorenberg, Robert Burig, David Wilson, Susan Retsky, Robert Cohen, Melissa Klein, Karen Benezra, Kevin Gray, Peter Ember, Ken Valenti, Cameron McWhirter, Stuart Miller, Amy Teibel, Sondra F. Shapiro.

When you also include a City Editor, Barry Abisch, Editors Fred Lowy and John Gambrill, and the 1990 crew of "female chauvinists" Editors, you can see the reasons why covering and reporting on a Village such as Port Chester was erratic, uneven, absurd, and far from having the staff worthy of a literary prize.

Many will say I hold a prejudice against THE DAILY ITEM. They may be right but you have to understand that after more than twenty years in public office, I saw the changes in the newspaper.

I most clearly can relate to the misunderstandings and feelings of ridicule I sensed by their writers, several of which were honest enough to tell me when they left THE DAILY ITEM that indeed it was conveyed to them to take sides and get certain officials. I suspect because of my verbal and written tussles with the news editors, they put me on a course that eventually would put me on their hit list. I was not endorsed too many times by the editors for my elections, however, I had won handily in most cases without their blessings, and I realize that it must have irritated them to know that Pete Iasillo won once again.

They showed their lack of professionalism at its best in my 1989 re-election campaign by not endorsing my opponent, Vin Sapione or myself. They instead chose to urge the electorate to write in a ballot and not vote for either candidate. This is the kind of nonsensical and absurd thinking that went on in the heads of its editors. They knew full well I was the better candidate, had the better record, but as the young people usually state, they "copped out" in their responsibilities as members of the fourth estate. With their vague reference in their editorial to my problems with the Landmark Building and their ethics probe clouding my vision, they high and mightily stated that I had "displayed a moral obtuseness" and "who knows when it will cloud his vision again." This is all bull spit. Why weren't they honest and related how Nancy Q. Keefe and I had words at my interview with the press and this was maybe her way of getting even? What really galls them is that I continually won no matter what they did to me throughout the year; such as never including photos of me at positive village events; not even in the "Almanac" section, clearly the opposite of what Chip Weil said in his statement, "A rededication to local news."

Their incredulous and sloppy reporting on the 1989 election was further proof of their lack of professionalism. The headline stated I had won a fourth term instead of a fifth. I told an editor, in this case, Nancy Q. Keefe, "You will not decide this election, the people will." I guess it was like rubbing salt in the wound. Maybe looking back I could have taken a more statesman like approach on winning and pontificated on what the future held for our Village, but one had to understand that taking it on the chin from people who really did not know Port Chester, its citizens, its problems, its hopes for the future, its anguish from the past, and constantly referring to my past problems was to my way of thinking, their way of "rubbing salt in the wound."

I will not go further on the problems I had with THE DAILY ITEM. We must realize that life is too short to be clashing with such people whose goal for their people was to improve the quality of life of its readers, rather, it would seem it was to punish and ridicule those public officials who would not cave in or step back from THE DAILY ITEM's so called superiority. Bernard Baruch, a wise and intelligent gentleman once stated, "Recipe for success: be polite, prepare yourself for whatever you are asked to do, keep yourself tidy, be cheerful, don't be envious, be honest with yourself so you will be honest with others, be helpful, interest yourself in your job, don't pity yourself, be quick to praise, be loyal to your friends, avoid prejudices, be independent, interest yourself in politics, and read the newspapers."

I wonder if Mr. Baruch would reconsider his last sentence in his advice to everyone. He might change that part of the last sentence to read, "Read the newspapers carefully, for their reporters and editors are human and subject to jealousy, envy, prejudice, and hatred." I have seen and read in the past years that the media relishes in dumping on those who provide public service with the idea that these people are either lazy or incompetent in contrast to the seemingly more well run private sector. What they are doing is demeaning a class of people who 95% of the time are hardworking, dedicated, and intelligent citizens, but insidiously the media are creating a loss of citizen self-confidence in their officials.

THE FIRST CAMPAIGN, 1970

How does one get involved in running for public office? I guess many people ask that question. There are probably many who would want to run for an elected position in their home town feeling they have the time, the maturity, the demeanor, intelligence, and ideas that qualify them to run. I'm sure many have been asked to consider running or as the phrase says, "Many are asked but few are chosen." Usually a person active in a political party is presented the chance, and deservedly so they should be given that chance. In my case, back in 1970, both the Democrat and Republican Parties presented the opportunity to me.

Ironically, the Democrats were first to seek me out. I was not active politically at all in Port Chester. I was somewhat well known because of my athletic achievements. I was active in many social, religious and charitable organizations, but never had I ever made any public pronouncements politically, except to second the nomination of "Ozzie" Zumpano at a Republican Caucus in 1968 when he was seeking his try as Village Trustee. Other than that, I never attended any Board of Trustee meetings or any political fundraisers.

In 1970, the upcoming April Village election saw the Democratic Party seeking a candidate to run with Democratic incumbents, Mayor Al Nencetti and Trustee Dom Bambace. On the Republican side, their Party needed a full slate to run a candidate for Mayor and two Village Trustees. The Democrats approached me first to run, however, they stated to me that they would need to get an approval from a review committee if I would be acceptable. In effect, they really meant that "Chappie" Possillipo had to give his blessing. For two weeks I heard nothing from them. The Republicans, on the other hand, through my good friend "Ozzie" Zumpano, approached me to run. Joe Dzaluk, a current Village Trustee, was already chosen to run as the Republican Mayoralty candidate and had enthusiastically endorsed my candidacy to run with him. In less than three days, the Republicans said I could have the Republican endorsement. Two days after my acceptance, the Democrats then called saying I could run as the Democratic candidate but I told them it was too late.

So now I was to be involved. Never in my wildest dreams did I ever figure this new adventure would last over two decades of ideas, pain, friendships, ruthlessness, and satisfaction. As we started to go forward there were countless meetings as strategy was planned for the campaign. Much advice and hard work came from "Ozzie," Irv Walt, the Village Republican Party Chairman Marion Granowitz, the Rye Town Chairman, and "J-J" Giandurco, a Village Trustee. Our opponents were Mayor Nencetti, Trustee Bambace, and former Trustee and Police Commissioner Nick Fasolino, a tough, politically smart individual. I admit that as I entered the fray that I was naive and not really attuned to politics, Village government or issues.

Joe Dzaluk and Dan LaDore, because of their political involvement in the Republican Party, really were more aware of what was to be involved in a political campaign. I asked myself several times whether my decision to run was really smart. I had for years become known in the Village as a "Good Guy," with a sense of humor, a hard worker on many campaigns for various charitable organizations with no scandal or enemies. This was all to change as we started the campaign.

The person who really gave me the encouragement to press on was my dear dad and closest friend, Casper Iasillo, Sr. What happened was that at a social function for a charity, my dad was approached by "Chappie" Posillipo and he advised my dad that my running for office was ill timed and for the wrong party. My dad, who was a really beautiful person, was so incensed at these remarks he told me the next day to keep up with the run. He gave me advice, loaned me money, and it was my dad who I always felt was my real hero that gave me the encouragement to approach this 1970 election campaign with great confidence and pride.

Running with Joe Dzaluk was a real eye opener. Joe left nothing to chance. Every move he made was well thought out. His ability to speak off-the-cuff was magnificent. A brilliant strategist, he cut to the heart of all issues and was well informed and able to sense the pulse of the public. Our first meetings, Joe, Dan, and I, dealt with what we felt were the main issues.

Joe felt urban renewal would gain for us the most mileage, plus to attack Mayor Nencetti's poor attendance record and his time spent at the Village Hall. Dan, more politically attuned, would confine himself to many issues, but really go after law and order and housing as associated with slumlords. I would grapple with the issue of drug use, especially by our young people and more use of up-to-date equipment for our Police Department. The campaign went forward with a great start as over 200 people attended our caucus at the YMCA. A well-respected and brilliant Republican, Anthony Catalano, brought my name forward to the caucus attendees. Seconding came from "Ozzie" Zumpano and Peter Gianukakis. My acceptance speech, my first try at a political speech, was somewhat subdued. What I said that night was: "Mr. Caucus Chairman, Caucus Committee, Mr. Catalano, Mr. Zumpano, Mr. Gianukakis, and friends, rarely in a lifetime is the opportunity presented to an individual to serve through elective processes his fellow citizens and his community. As a life long resident of Port Chester, I humbly and with a great deal of pride, accept the nomination afforded to me tonight by the Village of Port Chester Republican Party. As a citizen who is fully aware of the problems of our Village as we enter the new decade of the 70's, I feel that my membership on the Village Board, with that of my two running mates, we can finally bring to the Village of Port Chester new dimensions and young ideas that are so badly needed now and in the future.

I pledge that when elected, my every decision on the Village Board, I will keep in mind all the people of Port Chester and that these decisions will be for the good of the community and not for any one privileged group or organization. I sincerely hope that my membership on the Village Board will be instrumental in giving to this Board the feeling that common sense will finally prevail in all its future decision and, in a true sense, help motivate citizens to contribute more efforts to help our Village.

Various individuals have asked me why I should seek a post on the Village Board. These individuals firmly believed that being a member of the Board has lost all meaning of prestige and honor.

As I have told these people, I tell you tonight - it is my own firm belief that the Board does not give prestige to the individual, rather it is up to the individual to add prestige to the Board. I know many citizens feel that being a member of the Village Board is a thankless job.

I feel that thanks and self-satisfaction comes to the person in knowing that he is doing a job for the good and welfare of the community and its citizens.

Finally, in closing, there is my own immediate family, my mother and father, my brothers and their families, and these wonderful friends who have nominated me tonight. These fine gentlemen and my family have, by their endorsement and encouragement placed a definite trust in me to succeed honorably. I will sincerely strive to ensure that my every action will reflect this trust and encouragement and I will do my utmost to do nothing to disgrace this trust in any way, I value this above all. I will strive to make them proud of me, for my success and accomplishments will reflect upon them and I will sincerely endeavor to make them even prouder of this endorsement.

I go forward accepting this great honor bestowed upon me, pledging to be a worthy candidate, an able Trustee, and as a result, a much better citizen of this fine Village of Port Chester."

From that night we went forward, working extremely hard going door to door, ringing door bells, handing out "palm cards," attending every conceivable event, dinner-dance, party and social function. Money was in short supply, although Joe Dzaluk got the Republican Party to pay for billboards, our speech making was confined mostly to house rallies of which we had scheduled ten which gave us an opportunity to present our views to people in every section of the Village. This was also a time where THE DAILY ITEM had a reporter at every one of these gatherings. We were instructed to have our speeches typed, double spaced, and have a different speech for each gathering.

Covering our campaign rallies were reporters who were really knowledgeable of Village politics so that if you made a speech without facts, you were questioned immediately after the speech. It was harder to get away with any "crap" because you were monitored right from the start.

Reporters who were really diligent at their profession were Fred Furster and also Dorothy Friedman. It was obvious from the start that THE DAILY ITEM would not endorse Joe Dzaluk. Just weeks into the campaign, on March 7, 1970, THE DAILY ITEM editorial staff blasted Joe Dzaluk for his ideas as regards for urban renewal. Being naive as I was, I felt we were doomed because of THE DAILY ITEM's negative statements.

It was also in the 1970 campaign I learned that the people of Port Chester might read THE DAILY ITEM, but they surely did not respect or believe their editors.

The campaign proceeded with stories and headlines almost every two days in the newspaper. The people were certainly aware of the candidates and the issues. As Joe Dzaluk had planned, the issue of the mayoralty campaign centered on the urban renewal issue with associated issues attached to the renewal plan with costs rising at the marina that really got to those boat owners at the marina. Dan LaDore and I stuck to our game plan. As the campaign progressed, I was really encouraged most heartily by a club I belonged to, the Brother Anselmo Club of Holy Rosary Church. I had invited them to my home so as to solicit their help and support. Almost the entire membership attended. I briefly spoke to them with the theme being I needed their help as I realized their families and their votes were desperately needed. After my short speech, we all ate and drank and without me knowing, the hat was passed. As they all left, they presented me with $300 in cash for my campaign. I was very touched by their generosity and remember I had tears in my eyes as I accepted the money.

Charges and counter charges went back and forth as the campaign progressed. Our campaign effectively kept the Democrats on the defense. While they, the Democrats, should have proceeded on the offense with their ideas as the campaign winded down, the Democrats were more and more trying to answer our attacks on their record.

As Election Day, April 14, 1970, approached, all the political pundits felt we had a chance at getting Joe, myself, and possibly Danny in with close victories. Even a well-known political bettor, Charlie "Cheese" was taking even bets we all might win.

THE DAILY ITEM didn't endorse us, particularly ridiculing my ideas, especially as regards protective screens in police cars, referring to my ideas as placing "chicken wire" in police cars.

Election Day finally came and after two months of hard campaigning, many typed speeches, losing friendships, much arguing and much hard work by my wife, Gloria, and my children addressing and stamping envelopes (self stick and computerized labels were not in vogue at the time,) we all gathered at Mollica's Restaurant to await the results from each district. The tally board was set up and food and drinks were dispensed. The final rally the night before at the Aviglanese Hall, which was traditional for the Republican Party, gave hope and the idea that we may pull off a three-man Republican win. Pat Federico was ready to call the results. Pat had made several speeches in the campaign attacking Mayor Nencetti and was a big help especially in the Washington Park section of Port Chester.

Now the returns were coming in. As each district and the voting numbers were yelled out by Pat Federico, it was evident to those knowledgeable in political elections that we were all on our way to an astounding victory. I, being a political novice, was still awaiting the final numbers. As the final tally was given, we indeed had scored a tremendous victory and upset. My family was shouting, my dad instructed my brothers, Phil and Casper, Jr., to go to his factory on Beech Street and bring back brooms.

These brooms were raised symbolically to show a clean sweep. My dad was really ecstatic. Gloria hugged me and was in tears. It was then that the impact of this great victory sunk in.

Joe, Dan, and I, had beat the Democratic machine headed up by "Chappie" Posillipo and former Mayor "Red" Zaccagnino. THE DAILY ITEM quoted "Chappie" as stating, "I can't figure this out!" The screams, the yells really erupted as the three of us spoke to this wildly happy group. Even Charlie "Cheese" was yelling, "I told you so! I told you so!"

My remarks to the crowd that night as reported by THE DAILY ITEM were short. I said, "This is a big victory for Port Chester. We will have a better Port Chester. It is also a personal victory for me." I noticed many people who didn't endorse our campaign now coming in to the restaurant yelling and screaming with delight at our victory. You will always find these two-faced, weak people emerge in every political campaign.

The final tally showed Joe Dzaluk winner with an astounding plurality of 1,046 votes. My victory was with a plurality of 324 votes and Dan LaDore with a plurality of 268 votes. We had indeed accomplished a great victory.

So the 1970 campaign, the first campaign, ended in a flourish and a great victory. Pat Federico became the Village Clerk, Arnold Bernfeld became the Village Treasurer, Dom Pierro became Corporation Counsel, and Sal Summa became Village Prosecuter. There were many good times associated with the first campaign.

I went forward in service to my Village excited at what I hoped to accomplish and to fulfill my pledges made at those political rallies. Never in my wildest dreams did I ever think I would continue to run and win in many more campaigns or even think about one day becoming Mayor of my Village, although a fellow 1946 classmate at Port Chester High School, Joe Mainero, in 1946 predicted that one day I would become Mayor.

THE LANDMARK CONTROVERSY

A wiser man than myself once stated, "Mistakes are costly and somebody must pay. The time to correct a mistake is before it is made. The causes of mistakes are: first, "I didn't know;" second, "I didn't think." In September 1987, a mistake was made by several Port Chester officials in signing a contract to purchase condos at the Landmark Building (old Lifesavers Plant). I was one of those officials, and I have regretted it ever since. Even after these many years since the Ethics Committee's decision cleared the officials, I still hear about the Landmark condo sale both jokingly and sarcastically. It is a problem that I guess will follow me to the grave.

First Hartford, the Landmark developers, put up condos for sale on September 12, 1987. I had recently returned from a vacation and when I received a phone call on September 10, 1987 inviting me to come to The Landmark sales office and take a look at what was being offered for sale, I responded by visiting their office.

There were already people outside their trailer office lining up for the sale that was to happen in two days. I was very delighted by this great interest because I had viewed The Landmark Project as the "anchor" for Port Chester's development in that end of our Village. When I was presented with floor plans of units for sale, I guess the euphoria of what I viewed outside and the fact that I felt this was the ideal type of living residence for my single daughter who was living with Gloria and I was why I signed the contract and remitted the 10% upfront check. Then one month later all hell broke loose.

I signed the contract on September 11, 1987. By less than 24 hours we had opened a can of worms that for approximately one year brought nothing but criticism and ridicule to those officials and the Village. It also gave to me a vision of a cruel, deceitful media I really never acknowledged. Their attacks through slick writing and twisting of the truth were a real eye opener. Their use of a columnist with no reputation to hammer hard at the officials, especially the Mayor, brought to the forefront a cruel type of journalism to Westchester County as never before by a so-called reputable newspaper.

Utilizing staff writers Carol Hayes, Joey Asher, Joshua Peck, Laurence Hooper, David McKay Wilson, Editor Ina Meyers, and Bill Faulk, it was clear to me that THE DAILY ITEM was out to win a literary prize. It's ironic that what these Port Chester officials did was also done by another up-county community months previous but somehow the Gannett newspapers, which knew of this, never exploited that story. No, this was their chance to ruin Mayor Pete Iasillo. The scene was now set for the story of the year and the fall of a Mayor.

On October 2, 1987, Trustee Sapione called for an investigation of the sale of condos to the public officials. With his attorney calling for the immediate resignation of the officials because of "illegal and unethical conduct," it was evident that things would heat up. Sapione called on the New York State Attorney General to probe the sale. The office of the Attorney General stated at the time, "As long as State Discrimination Laws are not broken, developers can sell condominiums to whomever they like and that the Attorney General was not investigating the matter." However, this did not stop the headlines and stories. The Westchester County District Attorney's office was contacted, as were the offices of the United States Attorney and the New York State Commission on Governmental Integrity.

At this point in this whole mess I really started to worry. Knowing in my heart that I did not seek to profit by the purchase of the condo or act illegally, it was becoming more and more apparent that I was in a frying pan. The thing that upset me was that less than one week after there was a call for an investigation of the sale. My attorney at the time, Sam Lerner, had conversations with the First Hartford Partner's attorneys on October 9, 1987, twice during the week of October 12, 1987, twice during the week of October 19, 1987, on October 26, 1987, on October 28, 1987, and December 4, 1987 requesting that I be given the opportunity to terminate my contract. Unfortunately, the First Hartford attorneys refused to terminate the contract.

As one looks back on this whole matter, if they had rescinded the agreement, might this problem have ended? One can only speculate. Everything went crazy after the request for an Ethics Committee probe.

The Ethics Committee, a three-member committee, was hampered by the fact that one member, Michael Morabito, was very ill. The situation was not getting any better, especially when, sadly, later on Mike Morabito passed away. The two remaining Ethics Committee members, "Red" Zaccagnino and Chris Rocca stated that they wanted a third voting member. Judge Roland F. Berlingo, a respected citizen of Port Chester, was appointed as the third member. With the committee now in place, both Trustee Colletti and I urged the investigation to begin. It was also at this time it was learned that now, indeed, the Westchester County DA's office, the Commission on Government Integrity, and the New York State Attorney General's office were now looking into the probe. It was also at this time that Bill Faulk started his columns on the Landmark and most specifically Mayor Pete. Things really started to heat up. It was at this point that I started to believe what someone once told me, "The news can be factual but not truthful." Such was the case in Faulk's columns.

Then the legal games started. Those who requested an Ethics Committee probe now asked that the Westchester County Board of Ethics hear the case. A petition to the State Supreme Court in White Plains to move the investigation to the County Ethics Commission was asked for. It became more absurd when they also asked the Greenwich, Connecticut Ethics Board to consider hearing the case. Also adding to the absurdity was the allegation that even Trustee Mutino had purchased a condo, which was false. Finally, Judge Ruskin dismissed the petition, ruled the Port Chester Ethics Committee legal. Even the Westchester County Board of Ethics said, "We will keep our hands off the Port Chester case." Finally, after two months of playacting, subterfuge, unfairness, and clearly one-sided press coverage, the Ethics probe was to start.

On January 13, 1988, the Ethics Committee started. The absurdity became evident from the start when objections were made to have George O'Hanlon and Ray Falcon as attorneys for the Committee. It was absurd because earlier at a Board of Trustees meeting they had voted to appoint them as the attorneys for the Committee.

This was the type of foolishness that was presented. The press did nothing to exploit this foolishness. Instead, they continued to hammer away at the officials. First to appear as witness was to be the First Hartford Developers. They balked at appearing, and stated if a subpoena were issued they would seek to quash the subpoena. Immediately after receiving written replies from First Hartford to over 50 questions posed to them, the Ethics Committee again wrestled with the question of whether or not to try again to subpoena

First Hartford Partners. The next bombshell was from the Finocchio Carting Corporation accusing Joe Coletti and me of conflict of interest in voting for condemnation of his property, which housed a garbage business on Main Street. It was interesting to note in the story that appeared in THE DAILY ITEM on June 9, 1988, which highlighted Mr. Finocchio's accusations, buried in this story was the fact that I had, a few days after the Gannett story broke, told of how my attorney had on eight occasions tried to contact First Hartford to rescind my contract with them. This news was buried, it was not headlined and was to my way of thinking, further proof THE DAILY ITEM was out to get me.

I realize THE DAILY ITEM will pooh-pooh my claim. That was their prerogative since they probably felt the indicting of public officials was bigger news than the officials being cleared. But we are getting ahead of the sequence of events.

After some preliminary meetings of the Ethics Committee, rules were established as to how the investigation would go forward. It was evident that the plaintiff was out to harass the public officials and intimidate the Ethics Committee to make great news for THE DAILY ITEM. They relished what was going on and gave ammunition to Bill Faulk. In fact, I was told that most of Faulk's information was coming from the plaintiffs.

From the start, it seemed that the accusers were not out to seek the truth on this matter, but to create headlines. It was amusing to see at the Ethics meetings, members from the Yacht Club encouraging the plaintiff. It was obvious they would love to see the person they viewed as Public Enemy Number 1, Mayor Iasillo, get his royally. From the beginning the plaintiff's attorney wanted the privilege to cross-examine the officials, however, to the credit of the Ethics Committee, they stuck to the rules and would not allow this.

One point I do feel the Committee fell down on was having the officials testify first. We all knew that now the plaintiff would make his testimony based on twisting the testimony of the officials to suit his needs. This was just what Bill Faulk was doing. It was interesting to note that Nick Fusco who in his haste to start the Ethics investigation signed a petition presented to him by Vin Sapione and now repudiated the petition and claimed Sapione had falsely notarized the document. With this revelation, THE DAILY ITEM printed one story on Fusco's charges but never scolded or rebuked anyone for their actions in this matter. This was just another case of head bashing the Mayor and anything done by the plaintiffs was okay. After all, the paper would never condemn those people who were supplying them with twisted information.

February 17, 1988 was a big media night for the Ethics Committee. This was the night that Mayor Iasillo, Trustee Colletti, and the other officials would give testimony and be questioned. The newspaper had several photographers, flash bulbs were popping. This was a media event. Washington, D.C. move over, Port Chester was the big news. All of the officials testified openly, honestly; answered all questions posed to them by the Committee and what was heard did not vary from what they had already told the media. Once again THE DAILY ITEM covered the testimony of the six officials in a very small piece in their newspaper. Here again was the obvious. They would not balance their news coverage. Their game plan was still, "Get the Mayor and the officials."

The plaintiff's turn to testify came on March 9, 1988. Sapione's statement was clearly written by a legal person. As predicted, he twisted statements of the officials' sworn testimonies. It was obvious that he was not in an environment he relished. He was nervous, mixed up and uncertain. Then when Nick Fusco testified and gave his statement again repudiating Sapione on his signature to his petition, it was icing on the cake to my way of thinking. It was at this time that it was revealed that Fusco, Sapione and his attorney were questioned by the Westchester County District Attorney's Office.

That evening concluded testimony by all parties, including the Board of Trustees members not involved in the investigation.

It should be noted that in the March trustee election, Nick Fusco, a sixteen-year incumbent was defeated and Sapione's attorney also went down in flames. I sometimes wonder if this wasn't the Village's way of getting back at them for their getting this whole Landmark controversy started and the black eye it was giving Port Chester. Only history will be the judge!

Things at this point dragged on. Finnochio Carting appeared at the June 8, 1988 meeting. The meeting was short and Finocchio made outlandish statements, even to the point that there was significance in my buying a unit at Landmark to look out over his property. The June 22, 1988 meeting was longer. Again the question of how or why to subpoena the First Hartford principals was discussed again. On June 22, 1988, Joe Coletti re-testified, as did Mike Ritchie. Mike revealed at the meeting he had relinquished his interest in the condo and would not realize any profit, gain, or benefit by the sale to his Uncle. Finally, one of the officials did what Bill Faulk said should be done and guess what? THE DAILY ITEM, in an editorial, excoriated Ritchie. The reason simply put was that they could now, after months and months, see that their campaign of yellow journalism was not paying off. This was the last gasp on their part to rekindle the flames of prejudice and bias. The June 22 meeting was again officials testifying and answering questions. Chris Rocca's questioning of Mike Ritchie was particularly intense.

The next meeting was July 13, 1988. I re-testified, as did Richard Falanka,

Bill Summa, and Chief Grosse. Again the plaintiff's attorney tried to change the rules as set up by the Ethics Committee and made veiled threats to contact the media. It was obvious by this time that the investigation was winding down. On August 24, 1988, the Ethics Committee held the final meeting and it officially ended the public investigation of the Landmark condo sale. But this didn't stop THE DAILY ITEM. Through news stories and editorials they tried to stir up the pot but they failed dismally. The encouraging thing that resulted from this whole investigation was that development and interest in the Village continued, and at an even swifter pace. I had made up my mind that I would not let the Landmark condo case interfere with my plans for the Village's future.

On October 5, 1988, almost one year after the controversy began, the Ethics Committee made their decision. In a nine-page advisory document, the committee determined, with the exception of Chief Grosse, the other officials had not violated the spirit of the law. It stated that in Chief Grosse's case, it would appear he had "received and knew he was receiving and unwarranted privilege," which I disagreed with. True to form, the yellow pens of THE DAILY ITEM however didn't stop as they cranked out a story in which they got a Pace law professor to comment on our actions. The hypocrisy of this law professor, knowing only what he read from THE DAILY ITEM stories, was making a judgment call on a matter he was obviously led to make by THE DAILY ITEM.

The response by the public was gratifying. Most people questioned on the street by THE DAILY ITEM didn't even know what was going on for a year. One woman who criticized us was the wife of a Port Chester Yacht Club official and everyone knew what her response would be. Even Bill Faulk made a half-assed attempt to revive the controversy. He failed miserably. A month later staff writer David McKay Wilson tried to revive the case. He also failed. What did happen was that:

1. The Ethics law was strengthened.

2. THE DAILY ITEM, hopefully, learned that they failed in trying to get the officials and the Village resented them more than ever.

3. Approximately six months later in my fifth term election try, I bested Vincent Sapione handily. I won, he lost, THE DAILY ITEM lost, and Bill Faulk lost.

My faith in my Village was renewed after one year of slanted news stories, 310 pages of verbatim testimony, ten Ethics Committee meetings, and approximately 20 hours of open meetings. I thank my wife and family for their courage and faith in me, those people who prayed for me, St. Jude who heard me, and a Village and Ethics Committee who believed in me.

In conclusion, something must be said of the Ethics Committee members Chairman Anthony "Red" Zaccagnino, former Mayor and Chairman of the Rye Town Democratic Party, Christopher Rocca, former Chairman of the Village Republican Party, and Judge Roland F. Berlingo.

Their task to hear, discuss, and make a clear, sincere, and honest determination in this whole matter surely was as momentous and important for them as those officials being investigated. The Committee had to hear verbal abuse at their meetings, read slanted news stories questioning their honesty and seeking to disgrace and bully these members into making decisions to suit the newspaper's wishes and desires. The pressure on these three volunteer servants was tremendous. Their reputations and family names were also in jeopardy throughout that one year on notoriety and publicity. I myself did not agree with all of their decisions but clearly recognized their quandary and dilemma. The Village of Port Chester surely owes them a large debt of gratitude for their patience and courage. Unfortunately, they may be forgotten in this matter; however, they set a standard for others to follow should an ethics problem ever again raise its head in Port Chester. Hopefully, it will never happen again.

THE SECOND ETHICS PROBE

Does lightning strike twice? I had asked myself many times, "Could another ethics probe ever be leveled against me?" In my mind I knew of no incident that could bring one about. As I prepared for my final year as Mayor, finishing out my sixth term and thirteenth year as Mayor, I was looking forward to ending the term with aplomb, hoping that developments would finally come into being. As the new Board organized in April 1992, I felt that two of the Trustees were politically indoctrinated and not really considerate of our Village but were really geared to hindering me at my means.

Trustee Terenzi had carved his way to some importance in Port Chester because of the constant favorable reporting he received from Kevin Gray, an immature reporter whose agenda, it seemed, on THE DAILY ITEM was to make Sam Terenzi look good.

The other Trustee, John McCrory, was now set to avenge the humility and ignominious defeat of 24 votes in 1980 when I bested him, an incumbent, in my first run for Mayor.

This second ethics probe all started when I was asked by THE WESTMORE NEWS if I would stop at their office, that there was a matter that they wanted to discuss and it was better if I could meet them personally. I agreed and when I entered their office, I was ushered into Richard Abel's office. As I sat down with Richard Abel and Suzanne Sorrentino, I was asked to listen to a tape. As I sat and waited for the tape to play, I said to myself, "What the hell have I gotten myself into now?" As the tape played, the voice coming through was to my way of thinking, mine. As it was playing, they would intermittently stop it and ask me questions. Being an individual who confronts things head on, I answered their questions, not knowing that they had already started the writing of a story made to make me look criminal, made to disgrace me and my reputation and to sell their tabloid and make money at my expense. I was duped into a scheme and fell for it. Where I should have consulted my attorney, Sam Lerner, before speaking, I was led into a cleverly orchestrated trap.

I stayed for about a half hour, listening and answering questions. After so many years in public office, knowing the wily ways of the press, I was unquestionably suckered in an ambush. When I was to leave, I asked where they got the tape or tapes. Their answer, someone had dropped it into their mail slot. They didn't know who delivered these tapes. If anyone believes that explanation they must also believe in Snow White and the seven dwarves. These tapes, stolen from the Mayor's office, property that were mine personally, that were of thoughts I put to recordings over seven years ago, tapes in no way in which I conversed with anyone or taped conversations, were now to be exploited for financial gain and to get the Mayor.

And so it started. THE WESTMORE NEWS in three days headlined their study, "Exclusive, secret tape reveals political favors, deals" knowing full well that there were no deals, no favors granted. For over two months, there were headlined stories of supposed deals, which upon investigation by any reputable newspaper would have turned up nothing illegal. Once again my family would have to endure shame and disgrace because of a crime, a theft, which no one in the press seemed to care about. Did THE WESTMORE NEWS care who stole these tapes? Did THE WESTMORE NEWS know who the thief was? Had the thief met with THE WESTMORE NEWS? Maybe some day we will all have answers to these questions. And what about THE DAILY ITEM, that pillar of the Gannett news chain, who monopolize daily newspaper publishing in Westchester County, what did they do?

They followed suit and would publish a news story almost a day later after THE WESTMORE NEWS hit the streets with a headlined story.

How did the ethics probe begin? On June 17, 1992, I received from Trustees McCrory and Terenzi, a memo requesting a special meeting on the Board to discuss allocation of funds to retain outside counsel in a preliminary investigation on whether there had been a violation of the Village Ethics Code by the Mayor and certain members of the Board. Some interesting facts regarding this letter:

1. The original letter was sent to The Village Clerk, not me. In all their years on the Board, these two Trustees did not even know how to start an investigation.
2. From the very beginning, I felt their plan (McCrory and Ternezi) was purely political. When I made a public statement at the meeting in which I stated that both Trustees were doing this to further their ambitions to run for Mayor, both scoffed at that statement. In less than three months, both declared their intentions to run for the office of Mayor. Was I right?
3. THE WESTMORE NEWS story was published on June 18, 1992. The letter to me for a meeting was dated June 17, 1992. Fully a day before publication of the newspaper, they had probably huddled to request the investigation.

Every week after the first publicized story of the tapes, THE WESTMORE NEWS would follow up with a new slant or version of the first story. This weekly tabloid went for the jugular. They called their expose, "Iasillo Gate." Their humor was unfortunately obvious, get Mayor Pete and disgrace him.

After the initial headlined story in which THE WESTMORE NEWS tried to intimate that I was trying to do a deal with Fred Gioffre for a promised job with Westchester County in exchange for hiring Republican building contractors on the Washington Mews development, they headlined a story with a blue banner, "Exclusive," my thoughts regarding personal matters and Board personalities and my thoughts on their seemingly untrustworthiness to me. These thoughts had nothing to do with any schemes, plots, or intrigues that were illegal in any fashion. THE WESTMORE NEWS knew this.

Then the Ethics Board, with the pressure from the Ethics Commissioner Chris Rocca, asked the Board of Trustees for not only subpoena powers but that the Board appropriate funds to hire special outside counsel. This unquestionably was so ridiculous. Thank God the Republican Board members used common sense and voted down the request for subpoena powers to the Ethics Commission. Granting them such authority and power would eventually lead to uncontrolled use of power to not only frighten but intimidate any witness that was asked to testify, not only about this case but with future cases as well.

The exclusive headline story continued. First it involved Joe Mutino and then Nick Fusco. I called both of these former Trustees and apologized for any embarrassment I might have caused them and their families. Both of them laughed at the utter nonsense of these exclusive stories and told me that no apology was necessary. They fully understood the politics involved.

THE WESTMORE NEWS would not turn over to the Ethics Board those tapes in their possession. They claimed their first amendment rights to not do so. While that was high sounding, I did tell my wife that as soon as the case dragged on and their exclusive headlines started to bore their readers, they would turn over the tapes. Sure enough, it happened. In a statement, THE WESTMORE NEWS consented to turn over the tapes and guess who they turned it over to? If you guessed Chris Rocca, you were right. Now with the tapes in their hands and John Lese, John Branca, and Fred Gioffre volunteering to appear at an Ethics hearing, the scene was now set for a real dramatic get together. Since I knew I did nothing wrong, I predicted the hearing would be boring.

It was high drama the night all three men appeared between being sworn in, TV cable cameras at the ready, and reporters with their skinny pads ready to take notes for a sensational story. All three men denied to the Commission any deals being made. All three showed the tapings were only crazy thoughts by the Mayor over seven years ago and all three stated emphatically nothing was done. It turned out to be a boring, boring evening.

Finally, after three months, my turn came to testify. It must be told that before I was ready to testify, I had several meetings with my attorney, Sam Lerner, to cover what testimony was given by Branca, Lese, and Gioffre. We researched the dates on the tapes and it clearly showed the tapes had to have been altered since the dates of meetings were not sequential. The Ethics Commission also recognized this but did nothing or expressed anything to show that the tapes were altered. Sam Lerner proved not only his worth as a friend but especially as an attorney.

He researched and delved into local laws, state laws, old minutes seven years ago and newspaper clippings I had in my collection. He made sure that I was ready for the Commission's questions. Sam Lerner left no stone unturned. He was great the evening I testified.

The night I testified was clearly not the high drama hoped for. The audience was very sparse. One clearly noted evidence was the fact that the two individuals who initiated this political witch-hunt, Trustees McCrory and Terenzi, were not in attendance. In fact, they did not attend the meeting that Branca, Lese, and Gioffre testified at either. My testimony took about one and a half hours. I was fortunate in that Sam Lerner and I testified in a question and answer manner that really threw the entire Ethics Committee backwards.

By Lerner questioning me, it precluded the Ethics Committee from seeking answers to questions already posed to me by Sam Lerner. The Committee was stunned.

Sam Lerner's stating that the Mayor was to be judged on the highest standard of morality based on evidence "obtained by the lowest standards of morality" did not interfere with the Committee's already opinion that the fact the tapes were stolen did not affect them. Only at one point did I almost break down in tears when I had related to the Committee my health problems, my wife's health problems, and personal business failures that I had hoped I would not have to relate. That part of my life was extremely painful and stressful and as I stated to the Committee, "the taping was a way of venting frustrations that were happening in my life." The questioning ended with the Committee attempting to seek some ulterior motives in my meeting with County Executive O'Rourke and Tony Colavito. I testified, without being questioned, that I indeed did seek out these two men for assistance in obtaining County employment. However, there was never any deal cooked up to hire Republicans. The probe of Iasillo Gate ended. I now awaited the decision of the Committee. It was interesting as I awaited their decision that my thoughts reflected on the three Ethics Committee members and the "favors" I did on their behalf and wondered if they would remember them as they contemplated what was perceived as possibly illegal, yet unproven acts that may have been committed by me.

On March 10, 1993, I received a first draft of the two majority members of the Ethics Committee's reports and findings regarding the stolen tapes.

Members Zaccagnino and Berlingo stated importantly at the end of the findings, "The majority of this Board finds the tape is not competent evidence standing alone and further finds that it has been unable to develop any outside evidence to show that an ethics violation took place, and for that reason so reports the Board of Trustees." Chris Rocca didn't sign the report, instead he would issue his own opinion. I was leaving public office on April 5, 1993 and what they might consider doing did not bother me. So, after nine months, the ethics probe was at an end. The final question, "Who stole the tapes?" Most people put the blame on the person who cleaned the Mayor's office. Only time will reveal the thief.

THE WHITE HOUSE
WASHINGTON, D.C.

One of the most exciting and spectacular events that happened to me in 1981 was an invitation by the President of the United States, Ronald Reagan, to attend a meeting at the White House with the President and Vice President Bush. The effect of this invitation was, to say the least, astounding. When my secretary, Marie Fallanca, nervously and excitedly showed me the telegram inviting me, my first reaction was that someone was playing a joke.

However, after we called the White House and confirmed the authenticity of the invitation, the entire Village Hall staff was thrilled and overwhelmed. You have to understand that this was the first time a Mayor from Port Chester was ever invited to personally meet with a U.S. President. When I called my wife, Gloria, and the family was told of the invitation, everyone went wild with joy. After a day I calmed down sufficiently enough to get ready to go and meet the President and made my plane reservations.

Without a doubt, June 3, 1981, would be a great, memorable event in my life. Before I left, I had to give to the White House security personnel by phone, my birth date and social security number.

Everything was now set in place. I was to leave by plane from the Westchester County Airport.

However, the day before I left I noticed my only dark blue suit needed repairs. My good friend and tailor, Vincent Malvarosa, came to my rescue and took care of the emergency repairs and pressed it slick and neat. Vincent always reminds me of his help, which was indeed important. On the day I was to leave, I arrived at the airport very early, excited about this fantastic experience that I would be shortly undergoing. However, another problem arose. The field was fogged in. Time was running out as I had to be at the White House by no later than 9:30 a.m. It was evident that the planes wouldn't be taking off. I was stuck. What could I do? By now the sweat was pouring down me in torrents.

I know I said a silent prayer to Saint Jude, Catholic Saint of those people despaired of. Just then, a fellow passenger who also had to catch an early flight to Washington, D.C., said he had a car and was going to drive to LaGuardia Airport to catch the Eastern Airline Shuttle. He offered to take the first five who wanted to chance it. I said to myself, "Hell, I better chance it with this guy because the planes here at the Westchester Airport are grounded." So, a carload of six of us got in this stranger's car and we started the trip to LaGuardia.

It seemed as though we caught every traffic jam that morning, but by luck or those prayers to Saint Jude, we arrived at the Eastern Shuttle gate. Luckily the plane wasn't full and I got a seat.

I know I kept checking my watch and the time, hoping I would get in the Dulles Airport and that there wouldn't be any more problems to hamper my trip. I dashed from the plane at Dulles Airport to hail a cab.

Never once did I concern myself with running through the airport lobby even though I had suffered three heart attacks and running was definitely a no-no. Again, by luck or my prayers, I got a great cab driver. I often felt as we zoomed from the airport to the White House that he must have at one time been a race car Indy 500 driver. I remember as I got in the cab, in the front seat, I flashed a $20 bill and told him, "Get me to the White House in 20 minutes and it's yours." I gripped the dashboard and my knuckles were white from holding the dashboard so tight. But thank God, we got there with two or three minutes to spare. The driver was terrific; I was frightened.

As I entered the security area vaulting the steps two at a time at 9:30 a.m. in the old Executive Building, all the data regarding me was checked out on the computer, and I was directed to one floor up where staff members briefed me and 10 other mayors from across the United States. It should be noted that the staff people told me I made it with only five minutes to spare. The staff people told us what would happen and what would be discussed at the meeting with President Reagan. We were then walked over to the White House where security was really tight. At several checkpoints the staff person had to show our passes and explain who the mayors were. We were then brought to the President Theodore Roosevelt Room and the table was set up with place cards. I couldn't believe my eyes. I was to be seated directly across from President Reagan, imagine only 3 1/2 feet separated us. Seated to my right would be Vice President Bush. We all sat and first to come in was Vice President Bush. He greeted everyone and as he sat next to me he asked, "Where are you from Mayor?" I answered, "Port Chester, New York." He then stated something like, "Heck, I know where that is. It's next to Greenwich, Connecticut, and next to Barbara's home in Rye." I answered affirmatively and now we sat and waited for President Reagan. I took a deep breath as the door opened to our meeting room.

In walked President Reagan. You have to understand that this was a very exciting moment for me. Here I was, the Mayor of a small village, seated with mayors of Atlanta, Georgia, Dallas and San Antonio, Texas, and other large cities, meeting with the President of the United States. I said to myself, "God, what an honor." The first thing I noticed about President Reagan was his height, over six feet tall, his broad shoulders and chest and the jacket he wore, like a brown tweed type sport jacket. His hair had only a few flecks of gray, and his handshake was firm. As I sat across from him I marveled at his genuine concern for our communities and his ideas on how to improve the Urban Development Action Grant (UDAG) Program of which our Village had benefited with sizeable money grants. I found myself not nervous and spoke up clearly regarding the Village's position on his ideas.

As I look back on this meeting, it's funny but there is one thing that I remember clearly about President Reagan, the backs of his hands. That's right, as one gets older we develop those spots on the back of our hands, liver spots I guess they are called. The President had none. I thought to myself, "Boy he sure must use a lot of that Porcelana hand cream." The meeting ended after 20 to 25 minutes, and the President and Vice President left shaking hands with everyone. We were ushered outside and interviewed by many news and TV reporters. After the interviews, we all left. I took the plane home after I paid courtesy calls to our Congressman Ottinger and Senators D'Amato and Moynihan.

The trip home was exhilarating and my thoughts of this great honor finally started to penetrate my being. Imagine, Pete Iasillo at the White House with our President and Vice President.

I figured that was the end of the White House visits. However, in September 1981, I received an invitation from the President and Mrs. Reagan to attend a cocktail party on the south lawn of the White House. Once again the adrenaline flowed as I attended the event. Under a huge tent, music was being played by the United States Marine Band, all decked out in bright red jackets and shiny brass buttons. The hors d' oeuvres were great, and I also met a friend from Stamford, Connecticut at the party, the then Mayor Louis Clapes. The President and Mrs. Reagan were really delightful. The only bad thing that marred the party was a tremendous lightning and rain storm. The rain really came down hard.

There were two large holes in the tent that really messed up the lawn and some of those in attendance.

Finally, there was one more invitation to meet the President. What made this visit so much more happy and delightful was the fact that the White House personnel stated that this time I could take my wife Gloria with me. Truly this was the most delightful White House visit because it made Gloria so thrilled to be there.

When we got to the Old Executive Building and passed through security, I could see the excitement building up in Gloria's face. As we were led to the room where the President would greet us, her whole body actually shook in expectation of the President's entry in the room. As he entered and greeted us all, I looked at my dear wife's face. I thought she would cry at this great event in her life and I was so happy for her. After a short 15 minutes, he left and fortunately from our seating position Gloria shook his hand. President Reagan then commented to Gloria "What a beautiful red coat. That happens to be Nancy's favorite color". After this excitement, we were directed to a fabulous room where we all had tea and cookies. We were joined by a good friend from New Rochelle, Mayor Len Paduano and his lovely wife, and the tea reception really capped a great day for me and Gloria. Oh yes, we took a souvenir, several napkins that had the President's seal and the White House imprinted.

Of course, I was honored by our visit and the opportunity to meet President Reagan again, but again most of all for my dear wife, Gloria, who deserved such a happy moment in her life.

I don't know if I will ever be accorded the honor of again visiting the White House, however, I sometimes ask myself, "Why was I so lucky?" Memories make up so much of our lifetime and the pleasant memories of visiting that hallowed building, the home of so many great people, will live with me forever and ever.

First official photo of Peter Iasillo in his run for Village Trustee, 1970

Mayor Iasillo (right) signaling the start of the Port Chester
Bicycle Races. (1984)

Mayor Iasillo (far right) signaling the start of the First Annual
Port Chester Bed Races. (1984)

Mayor Iasillo in his favorite task, either ground breaking or ribbon cutting in Port Chester's move forward towards development. (1985)

Official White House photo of meeting with President Ronald Reagan and Vice-President George Bush (Mayor Iasillo seated right, center) (1981)

Annual Police Dinner (L-R) Joe Suppa, Dom Mecca, Joe Tassone,
Village Clerk Fritz Falanka, Jake Innominato, Mayor Peter Iasillo.
(Please Note: Four out of six have real moustaches.) (1983)

Police Conference Top Row (L-R) Chief Geldart, Trustee Iasillo
Front Row (L-R) Mayor Dzaluk, Supervisor Posillipo, Trustee Schmel,
Trustee Fidelibus. (1971)

Contract Signing for Fox Island Development.
Back Row (L-R) Trustees Gianfrancesco, Terenzi, McMahon and Colletti.
Front Row (L-R) Developer James Harvie, Mayor Iasillo and (unknown) (1988)

Ground Breaking Cuddy Community Park
(L-R) Trustee Branca, County Legislator Pierro, Trustee Sapione,
Mayor Iasillo, Trustee Mutino, Trustee Colletti. (1986)

Dedication of "Chappie" Posillipo Park (L-R) Park Commissioner
Terry Nugent, Mayor Iasillo, Mrs. Rose Posillipo, Rubino Family (1990)

Dedication, William James Memorial Park (L-R) Ret. Colonel Bernard Abel,
Congressman Joseph Dioguardia, Mayor Peter Iasillo, Mrs. William James (1988)

Vice President, Ron Shaw of
Pilot Pen, Sponsor of the First
Concert in the Park. (1981)

First Concert in the Park, Ret. Colonel Paul
Wickesser Leading the Port Chester Pops Band.
(1981)

First Halloween in the Park
(L-R) Trustee John Branca,
Mayor Iasillo (in costume),
Village Clerk Fritz Falanka
(1991)

John Rieches Completing the First Port Chester
Mini-Marathon, April 26, 1981.
Please Note - John has one leg.

Village of Port Chester Accepting a Check for $500,000 for the Mianus
Bridge Collapse. (L-R) County Executive Andrew O'Rourke,
Senator Al D'Amato, Mayor Peter Iasillo (1983)

Mayor Peter Iasillo Gazebo in Lyon Park (1989)

Port Chester Board of Trustees, 1983
(L-R) Trustees Nick Fusco, Brien McMahon, Ray Hellman, Mayor Iasillo, Trustee
John Branca, Gary Gianfrancesco, Carmen Talia (1983)

THE "YOUNG TURKS" I

With the Village election in March, 1989, and the total demolishing of the Democrats by a fired up Republican Party, the Village Board became a Board of seven Republicans. There was continuous yelling by the Republican Party loyalists as the vote became final that night at Marisa's Restaurant. Shouts of 12-0, 12-0, 12-0, ripped through the smoky room. The 12-0 indicated that the Village Board consisted of seven Republicans and the Town Board consisted of five Republicans. The impossible had been achieved; complete domination of Town and Village politics was attained. Everyone seemed to take credit for the night. Statements from those who worked so hard to make this happen, whose vitality and spirit brought this about. It went on and on. One thing was noticeable, Peter Iasillo didn't seem to be mentioned. Even Ray Hellman remarked to me, "When the hell are they going to introduce you?" I also wondered. After nine successful runs for public office, I really was standing back asking the same question. "Didn't I, after 19 years in office, have anything to do with this evening?" This should have been the first sign that the youth movement was starting. "Old war horses" such as me would be sent out to pasture. Even Joe Dzaluk whispered to me, "A complete 7-0 Board, I don't know Mayor if this will really be good for you personally." Judge Gioffre whispered, "Now your problems will begin." How prophetic those words were.

As he said that, I thought back to Ed Saltzman's remarks. "Too many Republicans on the Board would not be in the Mayor's best interests." Being a Republican Party loyalist, I reflected on my achievements as Mayor, and the help I had given to the six Trustees. I had lent my name, experience, and advice to enhance their campaigns. I had lent my name to bring in fantastic amounts of money to the Republican Party. I had also lent my name and prestige in both 1982 and 1988 to fundraisers to take the Republican Party out of the financial holes they were in, to beat back an ethics investigation and win an election impressively against great odds (especially the media). Hell, I felt I now had achieved the impossible and the road forward would be smooth and clear.

Wrong, wrong, wrong.

The rumblings started very slowly in March, 1989. It began with the selection of the Deputy Mayor position or as the Port Chester Ordinance stated it, President of the Board. I wanted Brien McMahon, but the Board felt Gary Gianfrancesco should hold that position. I could have made some problems on the choice because the normal and positive approach was to accede to the Mayor's wishes, however, because of reluctance from Brien to demand the position and my trying to have harmony in the party, I gave in. This was probably my first mistake. My thoughts at the time were that in 1991 I would retire from politics and not run, so why create a problem that really wasn't necessary? Gary Gianfrancesco got his shiny new Deputy Mayor's badge. (There was a definite affinity by Board members to having badges.)

With my thoughts of retiring in 1991, I was determined to look for a successor "to the throne" so to speak. My choice was Gary Gianfrancesco. Why Gary? I thought long and hard regarding the choice. Trustee John Branca probably could have been the ideal person as he singly possessed the heart and compassion needed to go along with the tremendous amount of work needed to effectively continue what I had attempted to do as a strong Mayor. I thought back to former Mayor Joe Dzaluk and his professional position at IBM hampering his job as Mayor. I felt that John, as an IBM employee, would face the same. The fact that Gary had his own business in Port Chester would afford him the best ability to spend more time at Village Hall which is necessary to continue the idea of a strong Mayor in council/manager type government. Brien McMahon was another good choice. However, being employed at the time by Westchester County government would definitely hamper him, especially in dealing effectively with the County bureaucrats.

All the other Trustees on the Board, Terenzi, Giorgi, and Rende, I felt did not possess enough experience.

So, I made up my mind that my swan song would probably be around January, 1991. I asked myself, was I being impudent in my choosing a successor? Why not! After over 19 years in public office and over 9 years as Mayor I felt I had, through my strong leadership, moved Port Chester forward toward the 1990's in a finalization of dreams and beautiful conclusions.

The time was right to meet with Gary Gianfrancesco and tell him of my plans.

We met for lunch on May 18, 1989. After going over items of great importance in upcoming Village projects, I explained to Gary what my future plans were, my schedule for retirement, what I had envisaged as how to politically handle my leaving, etc. Everything was fine. He was very happy with my feeling that he was the person to take up the reins as Mayor of Port Chester. I then went forward always making sure that Gary was aware of those items of great importance. Things were working out well. ...Too well I guess! Somewhere between that May 18, 1989 meeting and around September, 1989, some personal matters came up that made me have to change my retirement plans. I made it known to everyone that I would now run for re-election in 1991. I guess the mistake I made was not sitting down with Gary and telling him of my revised future plans. I suspect Gary had felt offended that my change of plans were not transmitted to him first. It was obvious that since our private meeting he was to be kept quiet until such time as I felt necessary. He had probably told his friends, family, and Village Board members. This was probably, to his way of thinking, a slap in the face. I suspect he felt ridiculed.

It was obvious from then that my days as Mayor would be days of "misery and woe." It started slow, but I sensed the hostility growing. More and more, my advice was not sought. My perceptions as to how matters that came before the Board might politically affect the Republican Party were scoffed at. My meeting secretly with the full Board of Trustees, which I instructed them was probably against the New York State Open Meetings Law, meant nothing to them. After all, they were a 7-0 Republican Board and who was there to challenge them? I determined there made no sense in having any more closed session meetings with the Board as they inevitably turned into yelling and screaming matches. They did their thing alone. Not meeting with them, however, was not my idea of good, reasonable government. The six of them were already meeting without me, setting up their own agenda as to how they wanted the Village to go forward without the Mayor as leader in any way, shape, or form.

It was obvious that Gary took over the leadership of the group with the group's consent. John Branca and Brien McMahon, who would have stepped forward and maybe stopped this, did not make me aware of what was going on. Brien on several occasions tried to make me aware of their meetings but was also reluctant at times in his conversations with me. His loyalty was very much towards Sam Terenzi, his running mate in the 1988 Village election. Sam was a forceful individual who somehow dominated Brien, a more rational and at most times, more peaceful individual. Add Brien's situation with his son, Brien Jr., needing assistance in getting through a Zoning Board of Appeals decision and it became a situation where I guess Brien felt Sam's more bulldog-like tenacity was more helpful as Brien needed the votes for his son's business. Things were not going well for me on the Board. I guess many people in the Village knew this. The younger members of the Republican Party were "on a roll" and old timers had better stay out of their way.

The November 1989 election for County and Town offices was starting up. Dom Pierro was in a race against Martin Rogowsky, a younger, more financially endowed Democrat. The race promised to be a difficult one for Dom. Throughout the campaign Dom made some glaring errors in political judgment that the media picked up on. His normal good judgment and vocabulary became bitter as the campaign went forward. His perception that he was being ignored by the young Republican Party people only made the race even bitterer. It was perceived that Dom had to contend with a well financed Democrat and a reluctant Republican Party. The result was ultimately defeat for Dom Pierro. Outwardly the Republicans took the loss badly. However, it was obvious that they gloated over this defeat. It reminded me of the election when Ron Tocci, a Democrat, was running for State Assembly against Fran Judge, a Republican-Conservative. The word went out to the Rye Town Republicans not to support Fran Judge. The idea was that we let Tocci win and after two years, we would beat him to again and take over the Assembly seat. That never worked out as Ron Tocci continued to win. The feeling I guess was the same with Pierro's seat. Let Rogowsky win and in two years take back the seat with a younger and more attuned candidate who was more conforming to younger people and younger ideas.

After this election, the Village Board now started to diligently become the group to lead and not the Mayor. The first big test came on a vote for a car wash application by Willie Marino. The application had gone through unanimous approvals by the Zoning Board of Appeals, the Planning Commission, Architectural Board of Review, and the Traffic Commission. This was probably the most talked about issue in the Village. Never in all my years of public office can I remember an application getting such unanimous support from all the Boards and Commisions in the Village. The important vote on the application was made on November 1, 1989. By a 4-3 vote

(Gianfrancesco, Rende, Terenzi, Giorgi against) Willie Marino's application was turned down. These four Trustees pontificated on their intelligence in turning down the Marino application. It wasn't a vote against the application, rather, it was a way of telling the Mayor that a new generation was in charge and I had better stay out of their way.

In December 1989, the headlines in THE DAILY ITEM read "IASILLO TRIPS OVER HIS COATTAILS," and referred to the statement by Julius Cesar, 44 B.C., "Et tu, Brute?" talking about his close political allies stabbing him in the back. The media knew what was going on. The 30-year old group was showing up the 60 year old Mayor. After accepting his help, advice, fundraising ability, speech writing, and press releases for their campaigns, the Mayor was now "a nothing," or as one Trustee stated, "a piece of shit." The insults that came forward in that December 10, 1989 news story were saddening to me personally, but were especially saddening to my dear wife, Gloria, who had also worked diligently for these Trustees and had to suffer the insults and ridicule as well. The statements made by the Trustees were very derogatory and incredibly insulting. They were made to belittle me and all that I had completed thus far in the Village's forward movement. The statements made me out to be nothing but a political hack whose main concerns were ribbon cutting and luncheons. It was made to seem that I was not concerned with the Village in general or in particular, the new wave of Village Trustees. My first thoughts were to enter the fray and respond to the insults but once again, whether I was foolish or not, I kept quiet for party unity. I knew that there would be a time to answer these insults. I reasoned to hold back and let nature take its course. (It should be noted that Willy Marino, the applicant of the car wash, died suddenly on September 15, 1990, of a massive heart attack which many in the Village attributed to the disappointment and aggravation caused by his turn down by the Village Board.)

The start of the new decade, 1990, brought about no better days for me. I was being punished by the "Young Turks." They continued to meet without me. I really didn't care because I knew that if I met with them I would only be pounced upon and I felt I didn't need the aggravation. The March 20, 1990 re-election for Trustees came. I was asked by the two incumbents, Branca and Gianfrancesco, to assist in their re-election campaign. Their Democratic opponents were Vin Sapione and Walt McClain, quite possibly the weakest candidates the Democratic Party could nominate. John and Gary were concerned and worried although in my own mind I figured they would destroy the Democrats. It would really be no contest. Weeks before Election Day showed the two seeking my cooperation, inviting me to photo sessions and using my picture and statements in their brochure. Everything was made to seem as though there was peace and harmony on the Village Board. There was, but only during the campaign. I related to our Village Clerk, Fritz Falanka; this cooperation was nothing but window dressing. When the campaign and election was over, we would find the Trustees going after me once again. Sure enough, I was right. About one week after this election, it was the same tactics. Pounce on the Mayor. In a story in the March 29, 1990 WESTMORE NEWS which headlined "MAYOR ANGERS VILLAGE BOARD OVER SENIOR HOUSING PROJECT," The Village Board went after me with a vengeance. Once again the ridicule, the innuendos and the animosity all came forward. The main thrust came from Gianfrancesco and Branca, who just weeks before were glad handing me, slapping me on the back and praising me and my policies in the election that gave them issues to run on and advice and counsel. I contemplated answering the story that was filled with vile lies. The statement I prepared but never submitted was as follows:

MAYOR IASILLO REPLIES TO TRUSTEE'S RASH STATEMENTS

On March 29, 1990, the Board of Trustees vented their anger again on the Mayor through the press, regarding my having discussions with persons interested in building senior housing the Village of Port Chester. At a meeting of the Mayor and the Board of Trustees on March 24, 1990, the question arose regarding an article that appeared in THE DAILY ITEM on March 22, 1990, regarding senior housing projects. I explained in detail how the article appeared but evidently when questioned by the WESTMORE NEWS reporter, after knowing the facts and being knowledgeable of the release, some Trustees instead felt the time was opportune to take pot shots, for Mr. Gianfrancesco to state that I "cut a press release." He knows this to be false and only reinforces the stories going around the Village that he is to get the seat of the Mayor. As to Mr. Branca's declaration that the Mayor's mode of operating is "unacceptable" to him, I am stunned by this remark because I have operated, very successfully since my election in 1980 as Mayor in the same manner. It has proven to be highly successful and the achievements made under my leadership were very acceptable to him as he ran each of his elections with facts and figures garnered by my "mode of operating."

It is also distressing to read statements made by the Trustees trying to create an impression that possibly my meeting with the developer would be construed as being illegal and border on the possibly that I am on the take. Branca stated, "There is a process in place that keeps things 'clean and open'". Gianfrancesco goes a little further and states, "It leaves it open to question about closed meetings and improprieties." Not having facts or the courage to say what they mean, they try to skirt around the issue with platitudes. Mr. Gianfrancesco also stated, "The Mayor would learn that there is more to getting re-elected than press releases and speeches" of which I agree, however, I run on my records of achievements, not on someone else's record. Finally, the threat from Mr. Gianfrancesco, "I will devote to his campaign everything he devoted to mine." Whatever that means, Mr. Gianfrancesco will have to answer, although it was quite evident in his last campaign he felt I could help him and Mr. Branca by inserting my picture in their mailings and including a special message from the Mayor. It is amazing that during the campaign they solicited from me advice, records, ideas, but once they won they reverted to becoming powers, so they think, in the Republican Party. It will be interesting to see how they will act to each other and the games they will play in their seeking of a way to dump the Mayor and who will win out, for they both have the taste to become Mayor.

It was comical in Gianfrancesco's closing statement in trying to become a statesman and not a politician by declaring, "This does not make for harmony." After doing the chopping, we then hear a statesmanlike remark. Once again, for party unity, I did not answer the "boys." My political experience and judgment told me to give them time and they'd be at each other like mad dogs. Sure enough, it happened.

The 1990-91 budget was now being discussed in April 1990 with its passage by April 30. It was now that the "boys" started to vent their anger on each other. At one particular "Executive Session," it was horrible to see these "adults" go after each other, calling each other the vilest of names and it seemed as though they would come to blows. Never in all my elective office had I ever witnessed such anger between individuals. I sat back and said to myself, "If there was ever a video tape shown how these people act, they would be impeached and thrown out of office." The ties that bound them; youth, ambition, and trust for each other were disintegrating fast. It now became a war. The sides were set up. Gianfrancesco and Rende against Terenzi and Giorgi. Branca flitted between both sides. I became an outsider watching what could later be the downfall of the Republican Party. It was then that I realized that a full Board consisting of one political party was wrong. There was no person to watchdog. Further proof of the breakup in their alliances came about through the Board trying to force me to create a new title for Gary Gianfrancesco. The title that they tried to foist on me was "Deputy Mayor for Development." Joe Rende, Gary's closest ally, along with John Branca, at the time tried to convince me that the title was needed and most importantly that if I didn't issue a release creating this position that they would bring it forward and create the new post.

It was at this time that Sam Terenzi, the current Deputy Mayor, started to have second thoughts about the title Gary and Joe Rende were trying to push. I made up my mind that I would not go for this title. When they, after a couple of weeks, saw that I would fight them on the issue and the illegality of the idea, they stepped back and came up with another title. This time it was "Mayoralty Assistant on Development." Again I balked and told them no way would I go for this title either. Using the Mayor's title in creating a position to enhance the professional career of a Trustee was not proper or legal and would aid the Village in no way, shape, or manner. I sat down in an attempt to settle this seemingly idiotic business of creating a title and put forward an idea of creating a "Select Committee on Development" consisting of the Mayor, the Deputy Mayor, and Gary Gianfrancesco who would serve as Chairman. Gary was against the idea as he felt it was not in his best interests to have such a Committee. In hindsight, if he had accepted this idea and a chairmanship, he could have really been effective in having the opportunity to meet firsthand with developers, bankers, realtors, business people, and moneyed people. Once again, because of immaturity on the part of the Board, my idea was rejected.

It was at this point that Gary got my good friend Sam Lerner involved. This upset me very much as I had always felt that Sam Lerner, a high school classmate, would always seek to assist me and look out for my interests. However, being Sam's office was in the same building as Gary's (Gary's father was the landlord), the two got together and devised another title. This time it was "Development Coordinator." On April 13, 1990, I met with Sam and Gary at Sam's office and they presented me with a five-page document outlining the position of "Development Coordinator." I was shocked that after 2 1/2 months they expected me to approve their idea at this meeting. Somehow I kept my cool and told them I would review their idea. I reviewed their ideas, marked up the copy and in less than a week later, presented it to Gary for his review.

In the meantime, I had been consulting with George O'Hanlon, our Village Attorney, seeking his review of the titles thus far presented. In each instance, he cautioned me against the adding of the titles. He agreed that the Board could create any position they wanted, however, if it in any way diminished the power or authority of the Mayor, it meant there would have to be a permissive referendum. The Board knew of this and that I would fight them at every step of the way if they continued with this insulting way of bypassing the Mayor's authority. Finally, after more meetings on this title, it was agreed upon by all and on June 11, 1990, the ordinance was passed creating a post of "Developing Coordinator." The "boys" were happy and as for myself, I had made the point that I wouldn't give in if it meant disgracing the Mayor.

From this point on it was a bitter struggle between the two factions as each group continually argued with each other. It was really that they now did not trust each other. Appointments to commissions were put off for months, The Village Republican Party effectively stalled these appointments and reappointments. It became a contest between both arguing factions as to who could line up their people on those important commissions to control what would go on in Port Chester. It was during these days that I particularly missed two important Republicans, "Ozzie" Zumpano and Argelio Rodriguez. Their stature and advice was sorely missed.

This part of those events regarding the "Young Turks" takes me up to September, 1990. In less than six months, if my health is okay, I would be ready to run for a sixth term as Mayor. A slight setback on September 2, 1990 of a mild heart attack slowed me up for a while, but my thoughts were focused on my next re-election campaign. How would these "Young Turks" act during my campaign?

YOUNG TURKS II

After a slight heart attack on September 2, 1990, my wife, Gloria, again showed her great ability to bounce back, answering the press magnificently whenever she was questioned about the attack. Fortunately, I got to the hospital very quickly and as a result there was no damage to my heart muscle. The stories going around the Village at the time were that the Trustees were having their rear ends measured to see who would occupy the Mayor's chair. Much to their chagrin, I survived. They knew the Mayor was here to stay and would run for re-election in March 1991.

Things started to happen as the fall season approached. The Draft Environmental Impact Statement for the Robert Martin Downtown Development Plan passed. As usual, Goldie Solomon objected. She was never questioned openly by any of the Trustees and especially not by the media. The problems of Trustees Terenzi and Giorgi and their recognizable efforts to get rid of manager Mike Ritchie surfaced once again. This time it concerned a piece of damaged Village Highway Department equipment, a leaf vacuum machine.

Terenzi and Giorgi were extremely vocal in their objections to repairing the equipment. I issued a press release which had the affect on showing up the success of owning and not leasing this particular piece of equipment. Terenzi and Giorgi became incensed by my statement. The division between them and the other Board members widened. The war was on. Terenzi and Giorgi versus Gianfrancesco and Rende.

I made up my mind that I would prepare for the March 1991 election by issuing press releases that would show Port Chester in a good light. These examples were: The Youth Bureau receiving an award, an on-ground parking lot downtown funded by a CDBG (Community Development Block Grant) fund, a recreation study, Halloween-in-the-Park, and the initiation of plans for the redevelopment of South Main Street. Terenzi and Giorgi voted against hiring Con Edison to work up the design for the redevelopment of South Main Street, even though money was appropriated in the capital funding of our budget to do so. They had originally voted for it. A blowup came up about when the vote showed Dan Colangelo voted for the plan. Terenzi, who by now was considered by the Board to be a handicap to Republicanism, blew his top at Colangelo after a meeting on the Town Hall steps!

He thought he had Colangelo in his back pocket and it infuriated him to see his plan of action collapse.

Towards the end of 1990, Terenzi again leading the charge, attempted to "get" manager Ritchie by claiming, through the Budget Committee, that thousands of dollars were being wasted through mismanagement in the Village Garage. However, he was now finding out the Board was fed up with him and his protestations. It even seemed that, although they went along with him, Giorgi and Colangelo were a little embarrassed by Terenzi's complaints. Then there was the attack by the Democrats on additional health coverage voted on unanimously by the Board. In attempting to save their behinds, Terenzi and Giorgi stated they didn't know elected officials were included in the passage. Their continual statements indeed played into the Democrats' hands and made the rest of the Board seem as though they were greedy individuals. It was at this time I prepared a statement that went to the heart of the matter. Once again, I held back so as not to embarrass Sam Terenzi, who by this time was really beginning to greatly annoy not only Board members but also many Village employees. The statement that I held back was as follows:

NEWS RELEASE
JANUARY 10, 1991

<u>MAYOR IASILLO EXPLAINS PASSAGE OF INSURANCE RESOLUTION</u>

IN A RELEASE TODAY, PORT CHESTER MAYOR PETER IASILLO STATED, "IN THE PAST TWO WEEKS MUCH MEDIA COVERAGE HAS BEEN GIVEN REGARDING THE SELECT COMMITTEE ON

THE BUDGET AND THE PASSAGE OF A RESOLUTION REGARDING THE COVERAGE OF VILLAGE OFFICIALS FOR OPTICAL AND DISABILITY INSURANCE. THE MATTER, BROUGHT UP BY DEMOCRATIC PARTY LEADER, GARY STRACUZZI, WAS, OF COURSE, BROUGHT UP SO AS TO CREATE AN ISSUE FOR THE UPCOMING ELECTION IN MARCH. HOWEVER, SOME FACTS NEED TO BE ADDRESSED AND SET STRAIGHT.

1. AS TO THE BUDGET COMMITTEE STATING THAT "THEY" WOULD TAKE THIS EXPENSE OUT WHEN THE 1991-1992 BUDGET IS DRAFTED IN MARCH, THE SELECT BUDGET COMMITTEE DOES NOT HAVE THAT AUTHORITY. THIS AUTHORITY RESTS WITH THE ENTIRE BOARD OF TRUSTEES. THE SELECT BUDGET COMMITTEE, AS DESIGNATED BY THE MAYOR, IS NOT A POLICY MAKING COMMITTEE, RATHER, IT IS AN ADVISORY GROUP SELECTED BY THE MAYOR TO MERELY CONSIDER PARTICULAR SUBJECTS REGARDING THE BUDGET AND, IF NEED BE, TO MAKE INVESTIGATIONS AND INQUIRIES WITH THE ASSISTANCE OF THE VILLAGE MANAGER AS OUTLINED IN MY NOVEMBER 21, 1989 MEMO TO THE BOARD OF TRUSTEES.

2. AS TO THE STATEMENT OF SOME TRUSTEES THAT THE ADDITION TO A RESOLUTION ADDING THE TRUSTEES WAS "AN OVERSIGHT ADDED TO THE RESOLUTION WITHOUT THEIR KNOWLEDGE," I TAKE ISSUE WITH THIS STATEMENT FOR THE FOLLOWING REASONS:
A. ALL BOARD MEMBERS HAD THE RESOLUTION IN THEIR POSSESSION AT LEAST SIX DAYS BEFORE PASSAGE, WHICH WOULD BE SUFFICIENT TIME TO QUESTION THE WORDING OF THE RESOLUTION.
B. VERBATIM EXTRACTS FROM THE TAPE RECORDING OF THE TRUSTEES MEETING ON AUGUST 1, 1990 INDICATE THAT NO QUESTION WAS RAISED AS TO THE BOARD OF TRUSTEES BEING INCLUDED IN THE RESOLUTION AND WAS APPROVED UNANIMOUSLY.
C. POLICIES OF BOTH THE OPTICAL PLAN AND DISABILITY INSURANCE WERE MAILED TO ALL TRUSTEES WITHIN WEEKS OF THE RESOLUTION APPROVAL AND NO COMMENTS UPON RECEIPT OF THE POLICIES WERE VOICED BY ANY TRUSTEE.

MY OWN FEELING IS THAT THE BOARD OF TRUSTEES ARE

DESERVING OF THIS COVERAGE. THEIR RESPONSIBILITIES AS ELECTED OFFICIALS INCLUDES MONITORING A $14.7 MILLION DOLLAR BUDGET, RESPONSIBILITY FOR THE HEALTH, SAFETY, AND CARE OF OVER 24,000 RESIDENTS OF OUR VILLAGE, OVERSEEING EVERY LAW AND ORDINANCE PASSED UPON IN OUR VILLAGE UNDER CONSTANT SCRUTINY BY THE PUBLIC AND THE MEDIA; THIS RATHER SMALL FINANCIAL EXPENSE ON THEIR BEHALF IS MINIMAL AND INEXPENSIVE. HOWEVER, IF THE ISSUE IS WHETHER OR NOT TRUSTEES WERE LEFT OUT OF THE PROCESS IN PASSING THE RESOLUTION OF INSURANCE COVERAGE FOR ELECTED AND APPOINTED OFFICIALS, THIS IS NOT SO. ALL TRUSTEES WERE MADE AWARE OF EVERY ACTION TAKEN AT BOARD MEETINGS. I HAVE ALWAYS SEEN TO IT THAT THERE ARE NO SECRETIVE OR HIDDEN AGENDAS TO CATCH THE ELECTED OFFICIALS, THE MEDIA, OR THE PUBLIC BY SURPRISE. I ADHERE STRICTLY TO THE NEW YORK STATE OPEN GOVERNMENT LAWS CONCERNING THE CONDUCT AND IMPLEMENTATION OF THE FREEDOM OF INFORMATION LAWS AND OPEN MEETING LAWS."

Should I have released the statement? I don't know. I do know that my trying to show the Board how to be more businesslike was becoming increasingly difficult.

It was in the beginning of 1991 that the Board, with recommendations by myself and Tom Farrell, passed the resolution to seek funds in the Community Development Block Grant (CDBG) Program. We had been very successful in each of our three-year grant programs. This would be the one that could set a new horizon for our Village. It would involve new housing for 40 seniors and 30 cooperative housing units for low-income families currently living in low-income apartments in both the Traverse Avenue and Purdy Avenue areas. The plan was dramatic and would show the Black minority that we did care for them. Terenzi and Giorgi did not speak too encouragingly about the plan. When the time came to vote on the plan, Giorgi voted with the majority, Terenzi was absent.

Things started to happen in January, 1991. The MTA was now starting to come forward with a massive parking deck and transportation center for the Village. This project, coupled with the on-ground parking lot at Willett and King Streets, would indeed provide sufficient parking for the future of downtown commerce. The Chamber of Commerce decided to honor me. Goldie Solomon objected. The biggest news was that Goldie would oppose me in the 1991 election for Mayor. The Democrats decided not to oppose me.

Opposing Terenzi and Colangelo were Democrats Angelo Rubino and Gary Stracuzzi. The Republicans would definitely repeat, however, Sam Terenzi would have a fight on his hands. It's amazing that whenever the campaigns started, although there was some rancor in the Republican Party towards me, they still looked to me to raise money, and 1991 was no exception.

The election was lack luster. I won, garnering 60% of the vote. Colangelo won big. Terenzi won but all agreed, he would have lost were it not for Iasillo and Colangelo leading the way and the Republicans spending over $15,000. This kind of expenditure was indeed shameful.

I had won an unprecedented sixth term. Having my granddaughter, Amanda, at the polls that night to witness my victory was indeed the greatest delight in winning. The newspaper had even said I had become a legend. Why not, when after all the crap they wrote about me that would indeed seem to kill any other candidate, I seemed to rise above it all and keep winning. The next two years in office would indeed be significant. The young turks had now made another change. Gianfrancesco and Rende lined up with me solidly and against Terenzi. John Branca continued his flitting back and forth. Rick Giorgi seemed to somewhat start to distance himself from Terenzi, but for how long I couldn't say. I would also have to start to think about whether or not this would be my last term.

THE YOUNG TURKS III

It didn't take too long after the 1991 election for matters to heat up again. The Board of Trustees started with the 1991-1992 Village budget. The internal meetings between the Board, in executive sessions (with no notification to the media,) were duplicates of budget meetings the previous year. The problem this year however, (1991), was that the Board directed the Village Manager to come up with a really "bare bones" budget. The Manager was necessitated to create a budget that eliminated possibly 20 to 21 jobs, an elimination of Wednesday trash pick ups, the Annual Fire Inspection Dinner, Main Street Christmas lights, two policemen, elimination of the Youth Bureau and six Park Department watchmen. The reaction by Board members was predictable. Trustee Terenzi yelled and screamed and stated "Ritchie's budget hits all key departments that everybody knows you can't hit." Giorgi and Colangelo commented, but their comments were almost placid. The Budget Committee seemed stunned. Their mouths didn't like the Manager's budget. They knew full well that by law the Manager is the Chief Fiscal Officer and must come up with a budget each year. The Board demanded a "bare bones" budget. Mike Ritchie gave it to them and now they were yelling.

Almost immediately the public reaction was loud and unacceptable, especially in the possibility of losing the Youth Bureau and Wednesday trash pick-up. The Budget Committee fought tooth and nail with the Board.

Once again the executive sessions erupted into name calling that by movie standards would be "X" rated. The constant persistence that they, the Budget Committee, which consisted of a C.P.A., a florist, and a mortgage broker, possessed infinite more intelligence than other Board members was amazing. One thing was clear, in my opinion. The Budget Committee never utilized common sense in their commentaries. During the meetings, both open and in executive sessions, I tried to remain above the immature squabbles by the "youngsters" and issued a memo to the Board after the concluded public hearings as to ways to modify the Manager's budget; to have programs be put back in the budget by priority. The budget, after much internal screaming, warring, and noise, was adopted by a 4-3 vote. I could not in good conscience vote for the Budget Committee's proposed budget changes. They were a political ploy for the 1992 election and not thought out with much common sense. Plus, if I voted no for the final budget proposals of Branca, Rende and Gianfrancesco, by New York State law, the Manger's initial budget would prevail and which I felt this was too drastic. The budget was adopted and taxes went up again.

Two weeks after the budget adoption Gary announced his candidacy for County Legislator against Martin Rogowsky. Again my prediction and thoughts came full circle with the election defeats of both Dom Pierro and Fran Judge. The young Republican politico's fouled out in ousting Ron Tocci. Would their plans for Gary Gianfrancesco work to oust Martin Rogowsky?

So, Gary announced himself. I pledged full support for his election for the County Board of Legislators. I offered to co-chair, with Chris Pierro, his initial large fund raising dinner. Gary accepted my offer and his dinner was financially a great success.

Press releases featured his name and not mine regarding economic development in Port Chester. I did not dispute this as I foolishly believed this would help his campaign.

Stories that appeared in mid 1991 told of great developments that would alter and improve our Village. Headlines told of the MTA parking structure, the facelift to South Main Street and The Robert Martin and Fox Island waterfront developments. The zoning change necessary for the Robert Martin Development passed without a hitch. The new storage center developed by the Arredondo brothers opened and a proposal came forward from the Larizza-Capocci Company to build 60 high-rise condominiums.

Then there came forward a report from the Long Island Sound Study (LISS) Committee that threatened to curtail all the plans for Port Chester's future. This was an important issue.

I led the fight and organized various mayors and union and labor officials to fight the LISS report. Here again was a case in point where a really important issue had to be addressed. Did the Young Turks respond or comment? Hell no! Once again they remained silent. The Village's future was at stake and they "clammed" up.

Around September 1991, working with the Westchester County Building Trades Council, I started a campaign to receive a $9.5 million dollar grant to build over 100 units of Section 8 type housing for seniors. Never in my wildest dreams did I even think the six Trustees would be against a project to assist our seniors. The ranting and intimidation by Terenzi and Giorgi literally scared the Trustees and important persons in our Village to remain silent or speak against such a needed project. Once again those Trustees slammed the Mayor stating that I went ahead with the project without their input. Again … falsehoods.

The election for County Legislator ended with Gary Gianfrancesco being defeated by Martin Rogowsky. Again the Republican political pundits were wrong. Gianfrancesco lost in Port Chester, his home town. This was definitely a blow to Gary who I must admit worked hard. He brought up an issue that was dead, that being the airport expansion. The Board of Trustees also cooperated by not bringing up issues that Gary would have to take sides on, especially the ZBA appointments. The idea was to not make waves. That night at Marissa's Restaurant when the election results came in, the Young Turks were once again defeated. They sure couldn't blame this defeat on me.

I could see that 1992 was going to be a bad year for me with this group. Then, in the early part of December 1991, the news was released. Rick Giorgi would seek reelection in 1992 not as a Republican but rather as an Independent. Two weeks later Sam Terenzi broke away as a Republican and became a Conservative. Here was what I had predicted. The Republican Party was breaking up. The youngsters had finally become tired of each other. As the Village awaited the next election in March, 1992, for the re-election of Joe Rende and Rick Giorgi, this election would definitely be a hell-raiser. Having the label of an incumbent was said by the political pundits to mean a loss for such incumbents. I didn't believe this, but no one on the Board spoke to me, communicated with me, or even recognized me. They were talking of "new directions" for the Village. What this meant was to remove Mike Ritchie and Tom Farrell and look closely at Fritz Falanka's role in the Village. In actuality, these Trustees, who felt they recognized the people and the politics of our Village, were only making a path for a victory for the Democrats. Maybe this would be to my benefit. If it happened, there would be three Republicans, two Democrats, one Conservative, and the Mayor. What a mix up!

WILLIAM FAULK

There came upon the newspaper scene in 1987, a person who effectively upset high ranking Westchester County officials to such a degree that the reputations of these officials, including myself, were in jeopardy. I remember writing a rhyme to describe this person but listening to advice of cooler heads, I did not submit it to the newspapers.

As I look back to the beginnings of his writings, he really had no reputation and no following. He was in fact a nothing in the profession. It wasn't until he hooked onto The Landmark story that his name became known. My problems and my name, recognition, and popularity in the County really propelled this nonentity forward and gave him the reputation he was seeking. There is a word in the dictionary that may closely describe his writing, and it also applies to THE DAILY ITEM in general. That word is "licentious." Its meaning, "careless of rule and accuracy, especially in literary matters; exceeding the limits of propriety."

Some Republicans referred to him as the "Daring Demagogue of the Democrats" for it would seem the only politics he "picked on" were Republicans.

In my political life I had been scourged and punished by the press, but never to the degree that this media person did to me. He naturally upset my family to no end. There was always the chance that after two decades of public service, good works, and a reputable family name in the community, it could all end. With the constant prodding by Faulk there was always the fear that he might intimidate the three person Ethics Committee. It was not a happy time in my political or personal life. It was very noticeable in my personal life, as so-called close political allies would not take the time to sit or converse with my wife and I. We were literally being ignored. It was particularly distressing to my wife, a beautiful, caring human being who had to bear up under the snubs from people she always showed care and concern for. I remember distinctly at an annual Town of Rye Republican dinner dance. Immediately after the speechmaking ceremonies all the people at our table left Gloria and I alone. They left in such haste. All evening we sat by ourselves.

Were it not for the Bernfelds, McMahons, Ray Hellman and Rekka, and the Pierros, we would have been totally alone. I told Gloria, who was very upset by this, "Don't worry, when I lick Landmark and Bill Faulk, the two-facers would come back." In politics, there are survivors. I was one of them.

From his very first column on Landmark, Bill Faulk unmercifully went after me. Bill Faulk was a clever little man, who with the power of the press elevated himself to over six feet in height by his sarcasm and caustic writings. His cleverness in writing was instead twisting the truth to suit his needs. Every column he wrote he more cleverly injected falsehoods together with known facts to weave a tale of subterfuge that somehow made it seem as though Mayor Iasillo, Trustee Coletti, and other public officials schemed together to purchase condos to make fantastic profits. Here this person who did not know me personally, never talked or interviewed me, was spitting forth his cleverly written venom, pandering to the masses, to their prejudices and passions and seeking the heads of public officials. Why? Well, I reasoned that THE DAILY ITEM was gunning for a literary prize since they put so many people on this story; five staff writers, one columnist, and two editors. With any luck a prosecutor might indict us and find us guilty of a crime, have us kicked out of office, maybe even get a jail sentence. THE DAILY ITEM, with their crew of propagandists would get their prize. Sounds foolish? To some it might be, but being in the limelight for so long, I truly believe this was the plot from the very start.

Cervantes wrote, "Truth will rise above falsehood as oil above water." But as this person wrote for over a dozen columns, I sometimes wondered if I could really believe Cervantes. From his first column he urged his readers to either call me at my Mayor's office to "give back the condo" or clip out a copy of his column and mail it to me. It was the start of a living hell. I received about 30 copies. He referenced to my not having a conscience and that I and the other officials had an inside deal with the developers and how we had voted to rezone the property to get a good deal for the condo. He was pandering to the masses that really don't trust politicians. These columns that twisted the truth were a real lesson for me.

If he was printing falsehoods, why didn't I write the ITEM to refute him? I did not because before his first column, I received a call from the editor, Ms Ina Meyers, asking for my side of the story. I explained my side of the story for approximately 20 minutes. When the editorial came out, they cleverly used about four sentences of my side and effectively made me look like a crook. That was enough for me to keep my mouth shut. It only proved to me that THE DAILY ITEM was out to get me, even if it meant twisting the truth.

One of the nice things that came out of this mess was the number of phone calls I received from constituents voicing their disgust at his columns and their belief in my honesty. It certainly was encouraging. I thought that maybe the Village residents had forgotten me, and my efforts on their behalf, but evidently they had not. Many told me of the prayers they were saying on my behalf.

A funny incident happened when two friends of mine, Deacons in the Catholic Church, Bill Vaccaro and Jack Munnick, prayed with me at my home to help me at this really bad time in my life. When they left, I was really uplifted by their prayers and sincerity. Well, the next day Faulk had a column that really roasted me, worse than ever before. I laughingly called the Deacons and told them, "no more prayers!" They weren't reaching the right person. We all had a laugh.

There were things reported to me with the idea that I could get even with Faulk. For instance, he was living in Mount Pleasant in an illegally converted apartment with no certificate of occupancy. When I called a political friend from Mount Pleasant, I was told they knew of it but were not going to make waves. There were stories of Faulk being stopped for DWI several times but covered up. With all this I figured it was best to just keep quiet and place my faith in the Ethics Committee, and hope and pray everything would come out all right. I remember meeting Faulk at one of the Ethics Committee meetings. He introduced himself to me wearing a rumpled blue suit and frayed collar, wearing white socks. He introduced himself and we had a very short conversation. I do remember when we parted he stated that if I was cleared he would write an apology in his column. My reply to him was, "That will be the day."

The column and apology never appeared. Today this "giant" of the news media I understand is a columnist for a NYC newspaper. I inquired of people how he was doing. The reply was, "No one likes him." That probably made Bill Faulk very happy.

It would seem that this person thrives on meanness and enjoys being disliked. What a poor commentary on a human being.

WILLIAM ROZMUS

There are many residents that come before the Board of Trustees, most of which give legitimate complaints, who inquire of certain Village ordinances and in general are nervous coming to the microphone to speak to the Board. There also have been those who appear without such nervousness, whose speeches to the Mayor and the Board are sometimes comical, bizarre, and indeed absurd. One such person who fit the latter category was Bill Rozmus, affectionately given the title of "Byram River Bill." His entrances to our meetings I think were timed to give some attraction or allure to his presence. He always seemed to time his entrance as the meetings were in progress. He would burst through the swinging doors at the rear of the courtroom, smelly pipe in his mouth, smelly dirty clothes on his body, definitely seeming that he was in need of a bath, saying hello to one and all. One evening he appeared as previously described but he was also carrying debris and driftwood that he told us he had fished out of the Byram River, stating he was attempting to clean up the river himself. Oh yes, I forgot to mention that he always seemed drunk. He garbled on and on until I finally had to recognize him to speak. He told us of the stuff that had to be cleared from the river such as crap, junk, and the favorite term of his, shit. People invariably laughed at this type of exhibition.

One evening he pleaded with the Board to donate a pair of rubber boots which he needed to continue his work. When we said we would give him a pair of laborer's boots, he became highly indignant at such an offer. Eventually I had him ejected from the meeting and he would always turn at the rear door when leaving and give a wave that always reminded me of Jimmy Durante waving his "Good-bye Mrs. Calabash Exit." I think Bill Rozmus holds the record for being ejected from more meetings than any other Village resident who has appeared before the Board of Trustees in the last 20 years. There also comes to mind the night we were having a Board meeting discussing the budget. Our courtroom was not air-conditioned. It was very humid that evening and only two 10" fans provided any moving air stream. In the midst of discussion, Bill Rozmus entered the room through the swinging doors and he was extremely ripe and smelly. Those in attendance naturally moved away from him.

As the discussion on Police Department funding was ensuing, Rozmus got up and started to complain about the food served to the prisoners in jail. He went on and on about the quality and quantity of the food, at one point describing it worse than shit. It was then that Carmen Talia asked the question, "How do you know so much about the food?" Rozmus answered that as a resident of the jail on numerous occasions he knew first hand of the food. At that reply, the room broke out in loud laughter. I have to admit, I broke up, with tears streaming down my face. Rozmus then went on about how bad the Police were which infuriated Carmen Talia. We though Carmen would jump out of his chair and physically attack Rozmus. As most times, two policemen escorted Rozmus from the courtroom and he gave all of us that little wave as he left.

I guess you could classify Bill Rozmus as a character. While obnoxious, he was harmless and one never got too close to him because of his smell and his panhandling, always seeking a quarter or a fifty center. I found out the only way to get out of giving him any coins was to tell him he already owed you money. At that, Bill turned away and preyed on other "clients." His entrances into restaurants infuriated the owners and I guess frightened the customers. At band concerts he was always bobbing and weaving as he walked. It was hilarious to see him backed up to a tree and as the music played, he slowly slid down the tree and ended up asleep.

Rozmus is not seen at too many meetings any more. Because of this, we cannot share in his brand of humor and absurd statements. This is one guy I will definitely never forget.

WILLIAM SANTORA

When I was elected in 1970 as a Village Trustee, the committee form of government was still in place. As a result of this, I was chosen to head up the powerful Finance Committee. As the overseer of the budget, the responsibility was enormous. In this capacity as Chairman, I also had direct supervision of the Building Dept. and its inspectors.

One of these inspectors was a highly qualified individual, William Santora, known to almost everyone in the Village as "Willie Cheen."

Willie was a master carpenter, which greatly aided him in his position as a building inspector. In those early 1970's we consistently heard the term "code enforcement." After almost 25 years in public office, code enforcement is still talked of as a savior of the Village. It meant inspecting mostly residential buildings and enforcing the state codes on safety overcrowding, rat and roach infestation, etc. This task fell mostly on the shoulders of "Willie Cheen." Between the two of us we set up a highly successful code enforcement plan that included inspections, follow up inspections, court appearances, fines, street by street inspections, etc. It was in the period of 1970-1972 that my involvement in house inspections with Willie really brought me an education and laughter. The first important thing Willie told me when going on house inspections with him was not to wear pants with cuffs. The reason was simple, so as not to have roaches taken out of the buildings by their nesting in your pants, in the cuffs.

I remember we inspected a two-family home at the corner of Midland Ave. and Armett St. (it has since burned down). Not finding anyone at home, Willie used a screwdriver to enter the downstairs apartment, which I thought was illegal, but was evidently done on many inspections. The steps to the upstairs apartment were littered with huge amounts of dog droppings. I did not go upstairs. We entered the lower apartment and I witnessed such a filthy, squalid apartment that I wondered how people lived in such conditions. There were dirty clothes piled in a corner, at least two feet high. Dirty dishes and cups were in the sink, with roaches having a grand old time.

Willie cautioned me against picking up any of the clothes. We went into the bedroom and Willie said we had to check the strength of the floor. This meant lifting up a very dirty and soiled bed about 18 inches off the floor and dropping it. When the bed hit the floor there were then literally thousands of cockroaches scurrying from all points in the room, from windowsills, molding, floor boards, etc. I immediately ran from the house yelling and screaming with Willie laughing very loudly. He had played a trick on me that I never forgot.

Willie would relate tales to me of some of his inspections, like the time he inspected a house on South Main St. Upon entering the community bathroom he found a bathtub filled with blood and the walls splattered with blood. He immediately called the police fearing that maybe a murder had been committed. After investigating it, they found out that one of the families in the apartment house loved fresh pork. What they did was kill piglets in the bathtub. As a result, there was blood all over the place. Another time we entered an apartment on Purdy Ave. where the stench of human excrement was overpowering. We entered the bedroom and there were pots and pans, cans and containers of every size filled with bowel movements. We learned the toilets were broken. The tenants felt that to get back at the landlord they would fill up the containers in a false sense of retaliation.

Willie's job was not easy. As with any building inspector he had to be diligent, professional, caring, and most of all be aware of the plight of both tenants and landlords.

Willie "Cheen" died suddenly of a heart attack while waiting for a train to New York City to testify at a hearing for the Village of Port Chester. I remember clearly that morning when Chief John Grosse brought me the news that Willie had died. I cried because I had lost a close and loyal friend. Those Friday morning breakfasts with Chief Grosse and Ed Saltzman, were somehow not the same anymore without Willie. I recommended that a ball field at Lyon Park be dedicated in Willie's name to recognize his contributions to our Village as both a building inspector and for his work in modernizing the Lyon Park ball fields. That plaque, along with one for Carl Schmehl is there for all to see and honor Willie "Cheen", a good buddy and loyal Aviglanese.

FELIX N. FIDELIBUS
Village Trustee 1970-1974

Being prepared for meetings with all pertinent information at one's fingertips is a task that most elected officials face must prepare for. Two of the Trustees who were best at achieving this were Ray Hellman and Phil Fidelibus. (Ray Hellman I will cover later on.) Phil was a man who was always prepared at every meeting. It was because of his having the right answers when the Democrats were in the majority that gave luster to an administration that really needed bolstering. When he was in the minority on the Board, his questions were probing, concise and really gave the Republicans fits. I attribute his background and education in civil engineering with always being on top of all subjects. I remember one specific incident that Phil made the Republican majority look amateurish. It dealt with a financial report being given by Village Treasurer, Arnold Bernfeld. You have to remember that at the time Arnold was new at the job as Treasurer. As a result, there was a great deal of gray areas as to where the Village stood financially. When Arnold gave the report, there was one problem; he had misplaced a decimal point. As a result, the report had problems. Phil Fidelibus almost immediately picked up on this and then started to expound on the shortcomings of this new Republican majority. He really did a job on us. Fortunately, Mayor Dzaluk, who was a master at picking up the pieces, gave some very detailed reasons why the decimal point was misplaced. For several minutes the discussion went on between the Mayor and Phil and to this date, I don't remember who won the day. Being a new, fresh, first-time Trustee on the Village Board, I quickly learned that your homework better be right at Board meetings. Phil Fidelibus was quick and sharp and did his homework well. If I had to rate Trustees I served with, the No. 1 position would have to be shared by Phil Fidelibus and Ray Hellman.

The 1973 election saw Phil defeated at the polls along with incumbent running mate, Carl Schmehl. This was really the biggest surprise to those who give learned opinions on elections. Literally you could have bet your house that Phil and Carl would win. However, as happens so many times, the unthinkable happened.

That defeat ended Phil's political life. He finally retired as Engineer for Rye Town and later the Village of Rye Brook. My final opinion, although Phil was a great Trustee, I really think he was never happy being in the public eye. But while he was, he did a good job. He really enjoyed his brief elected period in Port Chester, especially when he served as its Police Commissioner.

ANTHONY LAICONI
Village Trustee 1980-1981

With my election as Mayor in 1980, there was once again a vacant seat on the Board of Trustees. The Board, because of its political makeup, presented problems in appointing an individual to fill this seat until our next Village election in March 1981. If the Board could not agree on an individual, there would definitely be repercussions with future redevelopment. With three Republicans, two Democrats, and one Conservative, we could have problems getting a four-vote majority on many issues. A special election would have necessitated an outlay of Village funds and was not to my way of thinking prudent or wise, but was considered.

Fortunately, the Board recognized the importance in coming up with a person who would serve until the next regular election in March. I issued a statement in May, 1980 that we would have a person filling my vacant Trustee seat by June 1980, thirty days later. I felt the current Board recognized the importance of this matter but I had my doubts this pledge could be addressed. I asked each Board member to search their minds and consciences and come up with names. A month later, we met and many names came forward such as former Mayors Dzaluk and McCrory, Lou Passarelli, Fred Tedesco, Michael O'Connor and Salvatore Lucente. None could garner enough votes for the appointment. However, Nick Fusco, to his credit, came up with the name of Tony Laiconi. Although Tony was a registered Republican, those of us who knew him personally knew him to be an intelligent and very independent person. I immediately agreed with Nick's suggestion as I remembered Tony from our high school days when he was a fiery, competitive ball player for the Mamaroneck High School Tigers. His background in banking and finance was another advantage to appointing him to the vacant Trustee seat. It was unanimously agreed that Tony would fill the seat.

From the very beginning, Tony Laiconi was his own man and operated with one goal in mind, to see to it that Port Chester would benefit by all his decisions. He made it clear that he would not run for the seat in March 1981, and true to his pledge, he did not. Tony was a dynamic Trustee and it was clearly evident he was not on the Board to "play politics."

If he sensed a vote was to be taken to only benefit a political party and not the Village, he made it clear that he was not on the Board to get involved in political games. His knowledge and participation in discussions in 1980 were significant. He participated in probably the most exciting, rewarding year in Port Chester's history. The Village started to dynamically move forward. That year we started plans for the WOIC office building, the cable TV contract, the first UDAG grants, coastal zone management grant, Southport Mews, Kingsport, the Midland Industrial Park groundbreaking, the Midland Avenue extension, the appointment of a Village Engineer and Village Attorney, and many more new, exciting plans. Tony Laiconi played an important part in all these developments.

Tony Laiconi died tragically a short time after he left the Board of Trustees in 1981. In his short tenure on the Board, he showed me what being a Trustee should be all about. He had no axes to grind. He had no aspirations to higher political office. He didn't caucus with other Board members to have any special resolution passed or to assist any friends with special favors or legislation.

He was a good citizen who came forward to help his Village in their need, serving to the best of his ability and contributing enormously to its success. There are many who forgot Tony Laiconi and his less than one year of service on the Board of Trustees. I will never forget this wonderful human being and friend.

BRIEN McMAHON
Village Trustee 1981-1985, 1988-1990

I have found in my over twenty years of public service that many Board members have strikingly different personalities that separate each other from their actions on Board matters. Their voting on issues and their demeanor varied at each and every Board meeting. One Board member who continually demonstrated calmness, peacefulness, and a bit of nervousness was Brien McMahon. When Brien McMahon ran for Village Trustee in 1981, I must admit I knew little of Brien's background except that he was very religious and had a large family of seven children. He was very popular, especially at St. Mary's Church.

Through his friend, Joe Dzaluk, I learned of his decency and concern for all human beings. He was known for shaking hands and rather than giving a "hello" or "hiya" greeting, would instead give a "peace be with you" greeting.

I really got to know Brien, his wife Bea, and their children after his election in 1981. At the time, he was also caring for his mother, a very charming and beautiful woman. It was easy to see where Brien received his caring for all people. I remember when I was running for re-election; my opponent at the time was Bob Kancir. Brien's mom worked at Kaplan's Department Store and in her quiet, gentle way, campaigned for me. Brien related to me how his mother was trying to solicit from a customer her feelings about the upcoming election. She questioned the customer who she might be voting for, Iasillo or Kancir. The woman answered her, "Well, Iasillo is doing a good job, but I may vote for Kancir. He makes a real good roast beef sandwich." It seems that Bob's Deli and roast beef would garner Kancir a vote. Brien laughingly suggested that I immediately counter this by offering at our political rallies either a hearty turkey sandwich or a meatball wedge.

In those early days of my administration, in the 1980's to 1985, the composition of the Board and its makeup was definitely older in years. There seemed to be a better visualization of Port Chester's problems by the Board members and an attempt, even by minority (Democratic) Board members, to cooperate with each other and seemingly put politics aside.

Years later this would change drastically. Brien was definitely a team player, but not a follower, as some might suggest. He believed in talking things out, seeking peaceful solutions to a problem. He was never vicious or bore a grudge towards anyone. Early on when problems of the Yacht Club became heated and headlined in the press, Brien was truly upset by the situation. He found himself torn between the Village and the Yacht Club, of which he was a member. We had many conversations which clearly indicated to me that he was in a quandary and really did not know which way to turn on the issue of the Yacht Club and its lease with the Village. His concern was for the Village development plan on the Fox Island site, but how does the Village do it without hurting friends at the Yacht Club? He finally resigned from the Club.

More problems came forward by the 1986 election in which he and Carmen Talia went against a new faces on the Democratic ticket. Vincent Sapione and Joe Coletti were both fervent Yacht Club members who approached the campaign not as campaigners but as people on a mission or crusade. Once again the smart money was Carmen Talia and Brien McMahon mainly because of their incumbency. However, as it sometimes turns out, the non-incumbents won out, with Coletti winning over Brien by 18 votes, a big upset, and over Talia by 122 votes. Needless to say, there was shock in the Republican Party. Each Republican Party loyalist had a reason why we lost. In my estimation it was that the other side worked harder. The Republicans were too confident. It now meant I would have a four vote Democratic majority with two of them members of the Yacht Club.

The loss of Brien was devastating. He took it gracefully and was determined that the people had spoken and he accepted it. However, he felt hurt because he felt, as I did, that the Party just didn't put out the extra effort needed to win. In 1988, Brien came back to the campaign wars once again seeking to redeem himself and prove that he could win. Teaming up with Sam Terenzi, the Republican machine went into full speed and Brien won once again, winning by a plurality of 613 votes over the seemingly unbeatable Nick Fusco. But his term was short lived. He resigned on April 13, 1990 to take the post of Director of the Port Chester Housing Authority. This now left me with a Board made up of extremely young members with agendas of their own. It left Brien saddened by his departure as he really enjoyed being a Village Trustee. This was evident by the fact that whenever there was a function or festivity to attend, I could always depend on Brien being there with me.

CARL SCHMEHL
Village Trustee 1970-1974

One of strongest factors, I believe, in my getting elected in 1970 as a Village Trustee was my involvement and the publicity I received as an athlete in Port Chester. Sitting on the Village Board with me in the early '70's was another good athlete and buddy, Carl Schmehl. Carl and I had participated for and against each other throughout our younger lives in softball and baseball. Carl had a lot to live up to since his dad, Carl Scmehl, was a former professional ball player who played for a short time with the Detroit Tigers. Carl was a fiercely loyal Democrat and argued with his Republican Trustees, always seeking to gain one step ahead and embarrass any Republican administration.

His particular strong points on the Board were his knowledge for the parks and recreation programs in our community and also the Fire Department for which he served as the Commissioner of the Fire Department. There was one great capacity that Carl had and it was his ability to fiercely argue at Board meetings with Republicans. However, once the meeting concluded, he never bore a grudge and resumed his friendships. I recall at one meeting I made a public statement that attacked the two Democrats.

When I concluded, Carl replied in such a manner hinting that I really didn't mean what I said. He was right. I was embarrassed and it gave me a good lesson in controlling what statements I would always make in the future. Carl loved smoking big cigars and making Village employees squirm at public meetings if he felt those employees were not doing their jobs in serving the public properly. I remember one meeting when he tore into the Chief Building Inspector, Lou Buzzeo, for what Carl perceived as Lou's laying down on the job. He really did a number on Lou. Lou merely looked at Carl, with a pipe in his mouth, and nervously bobbed the pipe up and down in his mouth with sweat pouring down his brow.

Carl was defeated in the 1974 election, which was considered by political pundits to be a big upset. He never got involved in running for public office again. He passed away at a very young age from cancer. I recall that I saw Carl in Rye after he had received some radiology treatment, being wheeled into an ambulette just weeks before his death. He had deteriorated tremendously. His once robust, strong body had now changed. You could see that Carl was very ill. I waved to Carl and inquired, "How are you doing, Carl?" He replied, "I'll lick it buddy." I know I had tears in my eyes as the van left. Carl didn't lick the disease. I saw to it that one of the Lyon Park ball fields was named for Carl. In this way his name will always be remembered by the community he served as well as he could.

CARMEN TALIA
Village Trustee 1980-1986

Due to the tragic death of Trustee Dan LaDore, there existed an open seat on the Board of Trustees. To fill this seat in the 1980 election for this un-expired term, the Republicans had Carmen Talia running. The Democrats had a retired police sergeant, Sal Bambara, and the Conservatives nominated Gerry DiRoberto, a popular restaurateur. It was a hotly contested campaign that was watched closely by the political analysts because there also was the mayoralty contest between incumbent Mayor McCrory and myself. As the election turned out, I won, and so did Carmen who won by a comfortable margin. This created a Board of three Republicans, two Democrats, and one Conservative. A rather difficult setup for me as a new Mayor since my seat on the Board, by my election as Mayor, became vacant. That also created a problem that is covered in the statement on Anthony Laiconi.

From the very start as a Village trustee, Carmen Talia was indeed a force to be reckoned with. Very outspoken with a volatile temper, there were times when Board members grinned at Carmen's temperament because we felt he would someday leave the podium and physically confront people coming before the Board. But this temperament was not really the true person, Carmen Talia. He justifiably complained about certain things that didn't go right or matters that took too long to straighten out, but beneath it all was a person who really wanted to see good things happen for his Village. As a former Commissioner of Recreation, he was concerned that programs already in place by past Boards be continued and were funded so as to improve them. There was one department which Carmen zeroed in on and that was the Police Department.

Carmen really concerned himself that our Police Department was furnished with the latest equipment. He listened very intently to all arguments and suggestions by police personnel as to how to improve their department. By getting so involved, Carmen clearly could have put himself in a position of being used by police personnel. By an intelligent grasp of the department and its manpower and their needs, he was able to accomplish a great deal.

It was not unusual to see Carmen frequently at the police station or riding in a patrol car to see first hand what was going on. To Carmen's credit, a police squad system was put in place that increased the output of the department greatly. It enabled policemen to work as teams, recognizing each other's strengths and weaknesses, and accomplished a more close-knit police organization.

Probably his greatest accomplishment would be his recognizing and pursuing with great tenacity the problem of scofflaws, those people who were ticketed for various traffic and parking infractions and never paid fines connected with those violations. Carmen, to his credit, recognized the amount of dollars the Village was losing by not following up on these tickets and boldly called for a program to put this money into the Village treasury. The Board of Trustees was astonished to learn that the dollar amount was several hundred thousands. A program was instituted and through a tracking and computerizing system, the Village started to receive this money. As a result of this success, the Village under Carmen's insistence went about getting scofflaws through the use of the "French Boot," a device that when clamped to the front wheel of an automobile, made it impossible to move. These cars were later towed away and were only released to their owners on their payment of traffic tickets.

One funny story about Carmen concerned our attendance at the annual Mayor's Conference at Grossingers. At night, as was the custom after the daytime work sessions, most of those in attendance attended the nightclub. We were all at a table with our wives when the M.C. introduced the next act. It was a harmonica virtuoso named "Blackie" Schecter. Well, when "Blackie" appeared, to our surprise, he was Carmen's double. Same height, same weight, same hair and his movements duplicated Carmen's. Our table burst out with such laughter, it literally befuddled "Blackie." Those who were there never forgot that humorous evening when Carmen was the act.

Carmen won a full three-year term in 1982, besting Democratic candidates Anthony Meloni and Ed Sexton. In 1986 he was defeated for re-election.

Today Carmen and his wonderful wife, Ann, devoted their lives to each other and their children and grandchildren.

Port Chester owes a great debt of gratitude for Carmen's important vote he cast on May 29, 1980 for the Kingsport and Southport Housing Projects that started Port Chester on the road back to a better future. A man of great moral strengths, he was also a very loyal and dedicated Trustee.

DANIEL W. COLANGELO, JR.
Village Trustee 1990-1993

With a vacancy on the Village Board of Trustees created by the resignation of Brien McMahon, there now was handed to the Republican controlled Board the opportunity to appoint a Trustee to the Board. Several names were brought forward such as Bill Giacomo, Pat McNiel, Michael O'Connor and Dan Colangelo. The person who was pressing the hardest for Dan Colangelo was Sam Terenzi. Sam made no bones about it. With Dan and myself on a ticket for the 1991 election there was enough clout and popularity for Sam to tag along and be a winner. Once again Terenzi's vigorous and loud declaration of support for Dan won the day and Dan was appointed on August 1, 1990.

Dan had great success as a vote getter in his run for Town of Rye Councilman. His term on the Town Board was seemingly uneventful. His participation in town business was notably subdued. Coming to the Village Board would be quite different as Dan was to find out very shortly as I appointed him to serve along with Rick Giorgi and Sam Terenzi on the Port Chester Budget Committee. It was like throwing a cat into a pen with dogs. Although Dan had experience in finance with a background in banking, I think the pressure tactics of Terenzi and Giorgi overwhelmed him. To me it was quite evident, as it would seem to others that Dan agreed to every bit of disruptive reports put out by the Budget Committee. However, then again, it might be that Dan actually agreed with the Budget Committee reports, even contributing to them. After five months Dan was labeled with an Italian phrase "moo-shod" (phonetically Italian), which meant Dan was quiet, tranquilizing, and placating. Needless to say, Dan's actions and non-actions disturbed the other Board Republicans very much. His silence was deafening as Giorgi and Terenzi bellowed about tighter controls at the Village Garage, the incompetence of Mike Ritchie, and other budget and financial interests. Not only was Dan silent on the Village's financial questions, but was usually silent at all Board meetings. His participation on issues before the Board was nil and fellow Republicans complained to me about this silence. I assured them that Dan was an intelligent, well informed, loyal Republican, and when the situation rose for him to assert himself, he would step forward.

The election of Spring, 1991 came with Republicans offering for re-election Mayor Iasillo, Trustees Terenzi and Colangelo. The Democrats offered for Trustees, Gary Stracuzzi and Angelo Rubino, but no Democratic challenger for Mayor.

Goldie Solomon, however, came forward to challenge me. It was quite evident from the beginning that the Republicans would win due to their experience in government. However, most political pundits agreed that without Iasillo and Colangelo leading the ticket, Sam Terenzi could have been beaten.

After the election, the matter of the 1991-1992 Village budget was the issue zeroed in on by the media. It passed by a 4 to 3 vote with Dan voting with Terenzi and Giorgi which again infuriated his fellow Republican Trustees. However, I urged calm and caution to avoid a party squabble and proceed forward.

After the budget was passed, the Village tackled such issues as the South Main Street Redevelopment, a new Robert Martin Development Zone, the Greenwich Weigh Station, senior housing, harbor site, Volunteer Ambulance Corps, and the Larizza Housing Plan.

On all the subjects, Dan voted his conscience but was still amazingly subdued and quiet on the Board. There were some meetings that Dan only uttered a dozen words. The biggest surprise to many Port Chester residents was Dan's participation in the termination of Village Manager Mike Ritchie.

Many of us felt that the prodding of Terenzi and Gianfrancesco was the reason for Dan's vote to fire Mike Ritchie.

In late June 1992, a second Ethics charge was brought against me as a result of some recording tapes stolen from the Mayor's office. As Mayor, my concern was, how would Dan and Gary vote on the issue of this probe? Would Dan weaken and vote with Terenzi, McCrory, and DiRoberto? Would Gary, for personal political advancements, vote with Terenzi, McCrory, and

DiRoberto? The ethics probe was quite extended with Terenzi and McCrory going after my hide with a vengeance.

The other members of the Board knew that Terenzi's and McCrory's scheme and plan was not to obtain justice but to further their aim to run for Mayor in 1993.

In September 1992 the Westmore News released the tapes and the Ethics hearing went forward. I must admit that in meetings by the Board of Trustees, before the release of the tapes, Dan Colangelo was a stand-up guy who voted on my behalf and explained succinctly each vote he made.

After the Ethics Committee completed its formal hearings and before a decision was reached, after the pleading of my family and true friends, I announced my plans for my future. They did not include running for a seventh term as Mayor. My last personal dealings with Dan were on the committee to review along with Gerry DiRoberto the resumes for the post of OPD Director. While Dan was consistently a quiet, subdued person, he truly possessed a sense of compassion which is needed while sitting as a Village Trustee. Maybe Dan's way of quiet diplomacy was what's needed for our Village.

DANIEL LaDORE
Village Trustee 1970-1979

The story of David slaying Goliath is familiar to everyone. The thought of the little guy taking on the big guy or the bureaucracy has always instilled in many people the feelings of love for the underdog. Such a guy was Trustee Dan LaDore. Standing at 5'3" tall, thin and small of frame, weighing not more than 110 pounds, wearing thick, horn rimmed glasses, Dan in no way represented what he really was, an explosive and informed Trustee. Speaking so fast at times that a slight stutter would occur, Dan LaDore personified not only a caring Trustee but also a crafty politician. In 1970, Dan and I campaigned for the first time, running for the office of Village Trustees. We successfully performed our Alphonse and Gaston act for four campaigns. We appeared together in 1970 for our first political adventure at a communion breakfast sponsored by the K of C. The speaker was especially good that morning so at the end of the affair, Dan and I went to congratulate him.

I praised him on behalf of Dan and myself. The speaker thanked me but asked, "Dan who?" You see, Dan was behind me and my large frame completely blocked him from the speaker's view. As a result, Dan always appeared in front of me at various functions. Danny and I were perfectly suited as running mates and Trustees. We extensively did our homework, studying together all issues, preparing strategies and statements, working out plans when we were minority Trustees and conferring frequently to act together to pass new laws or budgets.

Dan tried to slay the Goliaths on two occasions (elections) and lost by tremendous pluralities. He took on the unbeatable "Chappie" Posillipo for Supervisor and then John McCrory for Mayor. In no way did these losses discourage Danny from goals he had set for himself. In fact, dogged determination in politics and government may have accounted for his failure in several businesses. Danny, who was never one to step away from a debate or argument, really suffered when he joined a group of G.O.P. District Leaders to try and turn the Republican Party around. From this he seemed to change dramatically. Possibly this was the start of his sickness, cancer. We who knew and admired him saw him lose weight from his already frail body. His finances were almost nil. Many of his friends knew of his money problems and went about soliciting, without Danny's knowledge, money to at least guarantee his family a happier Christmas. I will never forget the night Chief Grosse and I presented Dan with several thousands of dollars at his kitchen table. Dan accepted the money very reluctantly, tears streaming down his face.

He knew that his life was ebbing. With his loving, courageous and delicate wife Maryann at his side, he accepted the money. It was several months later that I had to give a eulogy at his funeral mass, the saddest presentation I had ever made. It was a little over a year later I again gave a eulogy for his loving wife Maryann. Dan and Maryann's five sons stuck together and today live happily with memories of their lovely mom and great dad. Finally, Dan's name will live forever in Port Chester as I proudly asked that the annual Port Chester Golf Tournament be changed to the Dan LaDore Memorial Golf Tournament. He was not exceptionally good as a golfer but he played as he did in politics, forcefully and with grit.

DOMINICK J. BAMBACE
Mayor, 1972-1974

Dom Bambace arrived on the scene as Mayor two years after losing a re-election bid for Village Trustee in 1970. With Joe Dzaluk not seeking re-election, the PIP Party fielded candidates for public office (Pat Federico for Mayor), which literally fractured the Republican Party. The Republicans gave Camillo J. Pagano, a marginally strong candidate, the opportunity to run for Mayor. The timing was right for Dom to seek office as Mayor as he had two young and popular Port Chesterites as running mates, Nick Fusco and John McCrory. The campaign in 1972 was a real barnburner. It was the type of slashing, rhetorical campaign that Port Chester unhappily was noted for. Dom, as most Mayors in the 1970's, was hampered by budget deficits and political fightings at Board meetings between Republican and Democratic Trustees. The politics of that era, the 1970's, unfortunately made our Village suffer. Political patronage was rampant. Village personnel continually lived in terror of being replaced or moved from supervisory positions because of political affiliations and because the Village was being run by staff people and not the elected officials.

Dom Bambace was a popular person in Port Chester but because of his highly successful insurance business, he most likely could not attend to the many problems that arose in the Village.

The position of Mayor and Trustee being part time positions hampered local elected officials. One incident I remember distinctly with Dom presiding at a Board meeting was a verbal confrontation between Dom and Monroe Mann. Words and innuendos flew back and forth until it seemed as though Dom had the upper hand. As Dom was making a statement, Monroe made an expression as through he were playing a violin as Dom spoke. Needless to say, Dom blew his top and only after he threatened to eject Monroe did he stop. The headlines the next day in the paper read, "Mann fiddles as Bambace burns."

It was in Dom's administration, to his credit, that the Village rezoned and set up for later development projects.

Our friendship continued and service to Port Chester by the Bambace family continued with Dom's son Gary, serving as Recreation Commissioner.

GARY GIANFRANCESCO
Village Trustee 1983-1993

One of the bright, young people to come on the political scene in the 1980's was Gary Gianfrancesco. He possessed the intelligence, background, and large family ties that could catapult him to the top in Port Chester's political history. However, he did not seem to have the ambition to move upwards towards the eventuality of becoming Mayor. He really didn't' show the drive or aspiration to one day take over the top spot. His early years on the Board showed an ability to understand and comprehend the problems besetting a not so affluent Village. He did what had to be done to springboard himself to win his election, but nothing dramatic that would endear him to the people. He performed robotically and achieved large pluralities and victories whenever he ran for re-election. Best of all, he was a loyal backer on the Board and agreed with what I was trying to do for Port Chester. Then all the harmony, loyalty, and understanding changed. Why?

Two things happened. First as I relate in a chapter, "The Young Turks, I", Gary in a meeting with me was told of my hopes of stepping down as Mayor and that I would like to "pass the torch" as Mayor to him. As I relate in that chapter, various personal matters came up that forced me to change my mind. It was quite evident that Gary was stunned by my change of heart about not running. I believe this was the reason for his turning against me and enlisting the other Republican Board members to start their revolution against the

Mayor. As Mayor, I had hoped that through my successes and great help in their campaigns that they would stick by me. It was evident that the rebellion against me had started.

Republican and Democratic friends warned me of what was happening. I guess even at my age I was naïve and brought up to believe that my leadership, which sustained a strong Republican majority, would continue to bring to me the loyalty I thought I had.

The second thing that happened was that Gary, I suspect, knew he needed one more Republican to complete the revolt. He found the Trustee that was particularly suited as a partner of change. This person was Sam Terenzi. Being of the same age and both looking to advance in politics, Gary found the ally he needed. Sam Terenzi was brusque, given to impetuosity, and would seem to do anything to get ahead. Gary needed for himself to play the intellect of this two-some, while Terenzi played the zealot. Their fusion was set and the play was to go forward. The big test came on November 1, 1989, when the vote was taken on the Willie Marino car wash application. I could not muster the votes to get this deserved application through, and the "Young Turks", led by Gary, held sway, and they did their deed. I was embarrassed, and saw clearly that Gary was now on his way. To where, I really couldn't figure out.

It's ironic that while Gary and the crew were doing their best to disgrace me, they still needed me for their re-election in 1990. In fact, Gary asked me to take an important role in his and John Branca's campaign. They especially needed me to raise campaign funds. Again, with my naiveté, I helped, hoping things would change at their re-election. They won and it wasn't three weeks later that they started all over again. It was clear to me and many other experienced political pundits that the Republican Party was on a downward spiral.

Gary finally announced his plan to run against Martin Rogowsky for County Legislator. As related in the chapter "Young Turks, III", he worked hard, spent much money, but lost. The Young Turks found out that they didn't have all the answers. After terminating the Village Manager, Mike Ritchie, by a Trustee group who definitely were not thinking straight (Gianfrancesco, Terenzi, McCrory, DiRoberto, Colangelo), and the later resignation of Tom Farrell, Gary then made his move. He probably recognized he didn't have the clear support of the Village to win another election, and that another shot at County Legislator Rogowsky would result in another defeat. He finally made his attempt at employment in the Village. He sought the position as Director of the Office of Planning and Development (OPD).

His seeking this position presented a problem. To be appointed to the position required the following:

1. He needed four votes to be appointed. He would have to resign his seat as a Trustee which left only three Republicans to appoint. How could he get a fourth vote?

2. He would have to show by resume that he was truly qualified, especially going against other highly qualified candidates.

A process was set up for myself, Trustees Colangelo and DiRoberto, and Tom Farrell to review resumes for recommendations to the entire Board of Trustees.

We received over 160 resumes which I initially reviewed and passed on to Tom Farrell to get his opinion and refer back to the three of us. Tom reviewed the resumes and we met to confer about his choices. You must remember, the two Trustees never saw all the resumes, just those referred to them by Farrell. I felt there were other stronger and more qualified candidates but said nothing and let the process go on. After we reviewed and interviewed the top candidates, we three agreed that Gary was not the best candidate. An applicant, a former State of Connecticut Planning Director, we felt was just what Port Chester needed. Unfortunately, at the last minute, he pulled out and left us at that point to put before the Board of Trustees five candidates, including Gary.

The interview process was held and as was figured out very easily, the three Republicans voted for Gary. The question probably on everyone's mind was why I would push for Gary after all he did against me. I suppose that as one grows older, the opportunity to "stick it" to someone lessens. I knew Gary's architectural business was going nowhere and I respected Gary's dad, "Baldy Joe," a good friend and wonderful individual.

I thought of his family and their needs and with all of this, I figured I would give him the chance.

Gary needed that fourth vote. You have to understand that through this whole process, Gary met with me on numerous occasions, continually stating the Republican Party owed him this position. I could have disputed his reasoning, but I felt why create another argument. Gary and I agreed that the weakest link in the other three Trustees (Terenzi, McCrory, DiRoberto) was Jerry DiRoberto. I implored Gary to seek out Trustee DiRoberto and plead his case. He agreed DiRoberto was the man to get the fourth vote, but would not seek him out. It was Dan Colangelo, Jr. that did it and sought out DiRoberto and in effect convinced him to vote for Gary,

Gary got his position as OPD Director, but one thing is still on my mind. Was this all a setup, with Tom Farrell involved, to direct the screening of the resumes to key in on Gary? They were very close friends, and I will always wonder if this was just a silly exercise in reviewing the resumes. You have to understand that the way it was arranged with the three-person review committee along with Tom Farrell, was a plan that Gary proposed to me as the best way to go about seeking an OPD Director. Was I set up? I guess I'll never know.

GERARD DiROBERTO
Village Trustee 1992-1993

When Jerry DiRoberto was elected by one vote in 1993, the consensus of many was that Jerry's win was a fluke and that he wouldn't add much to his role as a Village Trustee. He would vote along with John McCrory every time. However, his vote for Gary Gianfrancesco for the position as Director of Planning really showed his mettle and brought the wrath of the Village Democratic Party down on his head. Jerry, with his common sense and sense of humor, weathered this storm and showed to me an individual who truly had the good of the Village's best interests at heart. When I brought up the question of restoring Veterans Memorial Park, which would cost over $90,000, it was Jerry who led the dialogue on the Board of Trustees to approve the $53,000 loan to the Veterans Committee. His firm statements convinced the Board that the park should be restored. As I personally got to know Jerry in that one year I served with him on the Board, my opinion of him rose 1,000%. He took his role as a Village Trustee very seriously, attended all functions that Trustees were invited to, (the only one on the Board to do so), and proved to be a human being who really cared and was concerned for all of Port Chester.

It was only for a year, but the friendship and respect Jerry showed to me as Mayor was really appreciated by Gloria and I. How many terms Jerry will serve as a Trustee is hard to predict, but I'd warn any opponent for Jerry's

Trustee seat that they will have a tough time. Jerry, by his age and wisdom, possesses much common sense, a true love for our Village, and a feeling of pure joy at his service to Port Chester's citizens. While this account of Jerry DiRoberto is short, I'm positive you can sense my real respect and friendship for Trustee DiRoberto.

JAMES J. GIANDURCO
Village Trustee 1970-1972

If ever there was an elected official who really enjoyed sitting as a Village Trustee, it was certainly J.J. Giandurco. Known by almost every person in Port Chester and surrounding communities, J. J. Giandurco, with his unique brand of humor, made Board meetings almost refreshing. Due to his ability to answer constituent's questions in clear, concise statements or mix them up by being negative, then positive, then negative, etc., he was able to handle any situation that arose. He was a fiercely loyal Republican who never wavered, especially in his backing of Mayor Dzaluk.

Statements at meetings, such as referring to a particular constituent as "the greatest thing since sliced bread" really broke me up. While some people may have referred to J. J. and his buddy, Ozzie Zumpano as political hacks, this was unfair because never were there two people such as these two who served their Village with such pride and honor to the best of their ability. One of J. J.'s greatest accomplishments was as the Fire Commissioner. He saw to it that our Fire Department received the best and latest equipment. His efforts also started the Port Chester Golf Tournament over 50 years ago. This was later changed to the Dan LaDore Memorial Golf Tournament. J. J., in 1972, lost a re-election bid because of the split in the Republican Party. Because of this, J. J. never fulfilled a dream of 10 years serving as a Trustee. I shall never forget J. J. because when, in 1970, I became a Trustee it was J .J. Giandurco who helped me to overcome my nervousness. J. J. was certainly a credit to his Village and a great "Aviglanese."

JOHN BRANCA
Village Trustee 1983-1993

The mastery of Village politics by the Port Chester Republicans was indeed enhanced by the election in 1983 by both John Branca and Gary Gianfrancesco. The thing that was nauseating was the fact that not much credit was given by the Republican Party to my name being out front possibly having something to do with their victory.

John Branca was fast becoming an astute politician. Running my 1980 campaign for Mayor, I bested incumbent John McCrory by 24 votes, added much prestige and glow to John as regards his work by political pundits. He was tenacious and steadfast once he got going. As with Gary Gianfrancesco, I predicted these two could go far in politics. The only thing that could hold Branca back was, as with Joe Dzaluk, he worked for IBM and companies were frowning on employees involving themselves in local elective office. John's early years in elected office were marked by his wanting to be notified wherever the action was. He wanted to ride in patrol cars at night with our police department and to be called out no matter the hour to be with firemen at fires. As a member of the Port Chester Yacht Club, was really into recreational boating and fishing. While at the beginning he was a steadfast ally, he was more closely allied with Gary Gianfrancesco. This was clearly evident as they both ran together at each and every election. They seemingly set a pact, like two blood brothers, and more or less agreed on every issue.

John, as a Trustee, was an individual who promised everything to anyone who asked. Many times he got himself into jams promising things that were impossible to deliver, and I had to help him out to take care of the problem. Deep down I felt John was a very compassionate person. Would he someday become a candidate for Mayor? While he never openly expressed a desire to run for Mayor, he almost always stated that each election was his last. Whenever a meeting was held in the Mayor's office, as everyone sat on the couches and chairs around the credenzas, John Branca somehow always ended up sitting in the Mayor's chair behind the Mayor's desk. To my way of thinking, he desired to be Mayor very much so. It was too obvious to me and others in politics that John salivated to become Mayor. When the "Young Turks" started their takeover of the Willie Marino vote, John did not participate with them.

This however did not mean he was not on their side, as witness a story in the press right after John's successful 1990 election. John felt that the story on the senior housing project was somehow getting the Mayor headlines and not notifying his Trustees. However, they knew of the project. John even stated in the press that what I talked about did not keep things "clean and open." Again as always, at election time *use* the Mayor, after the election, *abuse* the Mayor. The question of appointing a Development Coordinator to the Board was heartily endorsed by Branca three months after the 1990 election. It is ironic that when John was elected Mayor in 1993 he said he didn't think it was necessary to have one. But I'm getting ahead of myself. In the last three years of John Branca's time on the Board of Trustees, he was virtually a non-visionary of any ideas. His contributions to the Board of Trustees were votes taken which I must admit were comparable to mine.

When I finally announced that I would not seek the mayoralty in the 1993 election, many people were stunned, others happy. Terenzi and McCrory felt they now had the chance of a lifetime to become Mayor. As one reporter stated, "Iasillo, the legend" not running threw the election wide open.

The Republicans sought out John to run and John again put on his coy act of not really wanting to run. Those who knew him best knew Branca was dying for the chance to be Mayor. The first poll taken by the Republicans showed Branca losing to McCrory by 5-7 percentage points. The Republican Party hired Tim Carey to strategize the campaign and plan and direct the campaign literature. Carey stated from the beginning that Branca's main opponent was McCrory, not Terenzi. All plans formulated were to key in on McCrory. This is very important to remember. Bringing in Tim Carey to run the campaign was also very expensive as Tim Carey worked for all the "biggies." This was also another indication that no matter what the costs financially, the Port Chester Republicans needed this victory. After losing two seats on the Trustee Board to McCrory and DiRoberto and losing the Town Council to Jim Sapione and a virtual unknown Eleanor Harris, it was clear Fred Gioffre needed this victory, *badly*. You might say his reputation as a political bigwig was at stake, plus, his boy John Branca had his head on the line.

Every week on Saturday mornings, before the election, strategy meetings were held with Tim Carey giving out proposed speeches, advertisements, and ideas. It was obvious from the beginning that my knowledge and impressions were helpful to move the campaign forward. I said to myself, maybe if Branca was successful, I would be recognized for my help. After all it was an election and it was "use" Mayor Iasillo once again. But maybe this might be the time the Republicans changed. As the campaign plodded along, it was clear that McCrory was still the lead horse. Terenzi continued to make his bombastic statements but was clearly going nowhere. McCrory was the real opposition. My statements in speeches and releases always stated John Branca was my right hand on the Board. I felt I had enough clout, especially with the seniors, to garner him votes. But something dynamic was needed to halt McCrory. Something needed was found and it can be revealed now that I found the way.

McCrory stated in some campaign literature and advertisements that he possessed an Associate Degree in Chemistry from the University of Connecticut (UCONN). I studied this and it seemed to me that McCrory never ever listed this degree. In my gut I felt it was a clear deception. I brought this up at a Saturday strategy meeting. They felt I was a little hyper and foolish. I finally convinced the Republicans to check out this credit McCrory was stating. When it was found out that I was right and McCrory was deceiving the public, this was the end to McCrory's candidacy. Fred Gioffre stated this was what made Branca's campaign turn around from a defeat to victory. The night the election returns came in, it confirmed Branca's victory. Cheers, yelling, and applause filled the room. Branca hugged Fred Gioffre and Pat McNeill. At that time I realized that "Mayor Pete" would now became a nonentity as far as the Republicans were concerned. Once again I was forgotten for my efforts in the Republican victory.

My thoughts in my final weeks as Mayor drifted towards how the new Mayor would handle the Robert Martin proposal, the Waterfront Development, the problems in the police department, the hiring of a Village Manager, the Mayor's hiring and appointing Republican cronies, and other issues.

JOHN F. McCRORY
Mayor 1978-1980, Trustee 1972-1978, 1982-1983

John McCrory was the bright hope of the Port Chester Democratic Party to start a dynasty that would equal the successful domination of Village politics that matched former Democratic Mayor "Red" Zaccagnino.

Upon winning the 1978 election by completely dominating the vote over Dan LaDore, John, with a clear mandate of the people and a strong Democratic Board, had all the tools necessary to start the turn around for Port Chester's financial future. Upon becoming Mayor, along with the Democratic Board, John dismissed Port Chester's first Village manager, Pete Pakey. Although the media and Pete Pakey stated he resigned, I know better. He was told to leave. This decision was hailed by many politicians and constituents as a bold step forward and Democrats looked for more of those spectacular decisions. One thing that hampered many of these political moves was the arrival on the scene of the new Village manager, Mike Ritchie. A true believer in a strong managerial concept of government, Mike Ritchie adhered very closely to the Village Manager Law.

This, I believe, started John's downfall as those in his party became disillusioned with John's inability to deliver. Party patronage started to wane and Democrats blamed John.

The Democrats on the Board cast a first defeat for John when they turned down his proposal for the Village to purchase the former Mulwitz Building

142

and turn it into a municipal building housing the Village offices and all its office personnel. I believe this was one decision that really irritated John and affected his attempts at complete leadership on the Village Board. His going forward and starting the process of urban renewal was commendable but once again, as with other Mayors, his inability to spend more time at Village Hall because of their full time employment, worked to the detriment of their re-election. It was generally perceived by the Village that Mike Ritchie ran the show and not Mayor McCrory. The timing for me to run against John for Mayor in 1980 was correct, although going against a strong incumbent who received the strongest endorsement I have ever seen by THE DAILY ITEM for a Port Chester Mayoralty candidate made my chances for winning the campaign pretty slim. Whoever won the campaign, with strong leadership qualities and a strong mayor concept, would reap the harvest. My campaign, after serving ten years as a Trustee and learning the game of politics, hinged on my getting across the point that I, and not John, had the strong leadership qualities needed to push Port Chester forward at a quicker pace.

Some say that John became complacent, read THE DAILY ITEM endorsement too much and irritated many powers in the Democratic Party. His seeming reluctance to endorse a senior housing project at the old Jewish Center did not help him win votes. Combine this with a strong Italian ethnic vote, and I bested John by a mere 24 votes, less than two votes per election district. John tried later running for a county legislator seat and was bested handily by Dom Pierro. Not as active politically today as in his previous years, John picks and chooses what elections to get involved in. As I told John in our 1980 contest, I really believed there were only two people at the time capable of running the Village, John or myself. Fortunately everything came together for me and history will be the judge as to whether or not I did a good job as Mayor.

Post Script: In 1992, John McCrory again came alive and ran for a seat as a Village Trustee winning with a huge plurality.

JOHN T. CONNOLLY
Village Treasurer 1977-1982

In 1977, with the seats of Joe Carlucci and Bill Davidson vacant the election for the two Trustee seats promised to be a wild and wooly election battle. The Republicans put forward Peter Gianukakis and Archie Drago, two very conservative candidates. The Democrats chose Michael D. Pierro and John F. Connolly. The election saw the Democrats blow the Republicans out of the water, winning with huge pluralities largely because of a fine gentleman, John F. Connolly. John was widely known and popular in the Village. The Connolly family had honorably served the Village for many years at difficult civic posts. John had served with distinction as a member of the school board and that service in such a difficult position gave John the background to serve the Democratic Party and the Village. At a time when politics were rampant in Port Chester, where decisions made at Trustee Meetings were most times viewed as political in nature, the meetings sometimes turned out to be circuses with charges leveled by individual Trustees against each other. With Joe Dzaluk serving as a minority Mayor, things could have been worse were it not for John Connolly. John showed his loyalty to his Democratic Party on all major decisions, appointments, and ideas. John, by his age and experience, conveyed to the public the impression of a sage and it was his quiet discussions on all subjects that really impressed the public. His problem in coping with individual citizens at Board meetings was something to behold. He handled each discussion masterfully. His reply to Serafino Guido is shown dramatically in my coverage on Serafino Guido found elsewhere in this publication.

It was John's wisdom which prevailed over his Democratic colleagues on the Board when they turned down Mayor McCrory's plans to purchase the old Mulwitz Building and renovate it as a Village Hall and government building. His vote against the idea pained John Connolly because he is a loyal person and to turn against his Mayor was somewhat distressful. Only history and those people who remember what happened that night, when the vote was taken, will judge if what took place was good or bad. The Village never really acknowledged John's important action, although I always make it a point to tell everyone, in seeing to it that the redevelopment of Port Chester went forward.

Several weeks after my election as Mayor in 1980, I arranged to meet with HUD (Housing-Urban Development) officials to determine in my own mind how our Village should proceed regarding development, and the role HUD would play in the whole scheme of things. I made the right decision as you will see later on, to invite the full Board which was at the time, five members. Of these five, Carmen Talia, Bob Kancir, and John Connolly, thank God, attended. We met in New York City at the Federal Plaza with HUD officials, led by Al Naclerio, who later was so helpful to our Village. The meeting started off with me pressing forward on what HUD had in mind for our Village. Al Naclerio, who arrived late at the meeting inquired loudly, "Who the hell are you? What the hell are you spouting off about?" When I retorted back firmly that I was the Mayor, Mr. Naclerio smiled and laughed. From that point on everything went fine. The result of the meeting, in essence, was if the Village of Port Chester accepted the two housing projects, Kingsport for seniors and Southport for low-middle income families, HUD would see to it that future plans for Port Chester's redevelopment would be met with cooperation from HUD.

The time finally came on May 29, 1980, less than one month after my being elected Mayor, for a vote to approve or disapprove the Blitman Plan (Southport). I felt this was the most important vote to change the history of our Village. A positive vote would mean the two housing projects would go forward and HUD would back us on future projects. A negative vote would mean the end of Port Chester. In a tension filled atmosphere that night, after hearing from Port Chester citizens, mostly voicing opposition to the Southport project, the vote was taken. Thank God it was a 4-2 positive vote. Nick Fusco and Bob Kancir voted no, while really brave Trustees Theresa Repaci, Carmen Talia, and John Connolly, along with my vote, voted yes. Carmen and Theresa were Republicans and listened to my pleas to vote yes, clearly recognizing the importance of a positive yes vote. The swing vote had to come from either John Connolly or Nick Fusco. I felt at the time Bob Kancir would not vote for it. John Connolly, by his vote, was going against the Democratic Party but because he attended that important meeting with HUD in New York City he realized the importance of the vote for Port Chester's future and believed as I did that HUD would follow through on their promise to continue to assist us. While I may get most of the credit for that positive action in May, 1980, plaudits should also go to Theresa Repaci, Carmen Talia, and most especially John Connolly for their bravery in not acquiescing to those voices of negativism and voting for the beginning of Port Chester's first big step forward.

After losing in a re-election bid in 1982, John suffered some personal tragedies and never again involved himself in politics. He re-married a very lovely and gracious person, Barbara and lived happily in Greenwich, Connecticut. Some day the Village will recognize John and other (3) Board members who voted their conscience and not politics at that May 29, 1980 meeting that literally changed the course of Port Chester's future.

JOSEPH COLETTI
Village Trustee 1986-1989

With the upset victory in 1986 by Vin Sapione and Joe Coletti over incumbents Brien McMahon and Carmen Talia, not only did the Democrats gain majority control over the Board of Trustees, but most significantly the two new Village Trustees were outspoken and dedicated members of the Yacht Club. It was expected that they would carry forward the banner for their Club members. What was expected of them came to pass.

Joe Coletti, a computer specialist, was not new to politics. In 1985 when it looked as though the Democrats would not oppose me for Mayor, Joe on the last day allowed by New York State Election Law filed a petition to oppose me. His party name was the Justice Independent Party. Naturally, several days later the Democrats endorsed Joe for Mayor. The issue of note in that campaign was the waterfront and its development and the Yacht Club. The election results showed me besting Joe by 1,551 votes, a very encouraging victory for me. But that was 1985. In 1986, Joe, along with Vin Sapione with their election victory, did what was expected by almost anyone involved in politics; they forcefully came forward to expound on their views, especially as regards the Yacht Club, the waterfront and the Robert Martin Plan (RMC). With encouragement from the Yacht Club, advice from the Corporation Counsel and a seemingly quiet attitude by the other Democratic Board members, Joe and Vinny became loud and vocal, especially against RMC and their Downtown Redevelopment Plan. Claiming that the Board of Trustees acted illegally in ratifying an agreement with RMC, Joe and Vinny, loudly opposed the RMC Plan. Encouragement to battle the plan also came from a group of merchants, who by the initial RMC Plan would have been displaced. It was at this time the other Democrats on the Board, Fusco and Mutino, realized that the obstructionist views of their two Board members might kill the RMC Plan. With my encouragement, the Board issued a joint statement condemning Joe and Vinny for reckless and unsubstantiated charges against the Board and RMC. With the resignation of the Corporation Counsel, who it would seem was directing the two dissidents. The possibility became that RMC might withdraw from Port Chester and a lawsuit might be filed by those merchants who would be affected by the initial RMC Plan. Things were really heating up in Village government and politics.

In less than a year, Joe changed his ideas and attitude. Probably sensing that an obstructionist attitude would not only harm the Village he served but possibly the future of all its citizens for many years to come, Joe changed and it was obvious at our Board meetings that he and Vinny Sapione were on a collision course. The confrontations between the two of them became more personal. As a result of Joe's supporting development plans for not only RMC but also the waterfront plan, Joe was now being ostracized by the Yacht Club. It was then in late 1987 The Landmark investigation began. A very well publicized action brought forward by Vinny Sapione and encouraged by the former Corporation Counsel gave both the Village and several officials a real "black eye." (The Landmark issue is covered in another part of this book.) The case placed a tremendous strain on Joe, his family, and personal life. Since I also was involved in the case, Joe and I conferred more and more. The ethics issue and its probe continued on for almost a year. The press and most specifically THE DAILY ITEM, its editors and a journalist, Bill Faulk, put an amazing amount of press coverage on the issue. Fortunately, the Board of Ethics was not pressured or intimidated by the media. Joe and I were cleared, but it did put a strain on many of us involved in the whole mess.

In 1989, Joe, because of business interests chose not to seek re-election. In my opinion, if he did run, he would have been victorious. He did participate in the campaign by signing a document along with Nick Fusco berating and giving facts why Vin Sapione should not be elected Mayor. It can now be revealed, it was my plan to have the letter drawn up. In the letter were my thoughts and words which Nick and Joe signed. I was re-elected. My hope is to someday see Joe Coletti again involved in Port Chester government, either as an elected official or in an appointive Commission post.

There is still much that Joe can continue to offer to bring Port Chester forward.

JOSEPH DZALUK
Mayor 1970-1972, 1974-1978

Joe Dzaluk, or the Polish Prince as I lovingly referred to him, was probably the most academically intelligent Mayor I ever served with. He possessed the kind of intellect that enabled him to think fast and respond quickly to questions and inquiries posed to him by both the media and his constituents. He had marvelous ideas for the redevelopment of Port Chester, such as the 30-story, hi-rise office/residential building at the Marina parking lot. His choosing not to seek re-election after his first term literally ended the Marina Project. The one big issue I disagreed with Joe was his abandonment of seeking city status for Port Chester. He was under great pressure on this issue and Board meetings were supercharged as Joe defended the Village's position on city status. The amount of yelling, charges and countercharges leveled at Mayor Dzaluk and those supporting Board members was unbelievable.

Mayor Dzaluk had very loyal Republican Trustees serving with him on the Village Board. Their backing enabled Joe to withstand the many problems the Village encountered in those early 1970's.

Joe showed his class as Mayor when a particularly tragic event happened, the Gulliver Disco Fire. This horrible incident was carried by the national media with newspapers, TV coverage, radio, and focused on the many deaths of the young people at this disco and whether or not Port Chester building inspectors failed to make the necessary inspections that might have prevented this tragedy. In our Village courtroom, filled with reporters, TV cameras, and huge floodlights, reporters yelled questions in quick succession to Joe. The pressure on Joe to reply quickly and responsibly was very demanding. The Mayor, with a great deal of clarity and having the right answers and visibly unshaken made our Village look better than the media was trying to paint us.

Then, there were also the fun things that I remember about Mayor Joe. Campaigning in 1970 with Joe and Dan LaDore was a great experience and also the happiest campaign I ever went through. One humorous event was when Joe and I went door to door and a woman clad in a flimsy negligee opened her door. Her dog sprung forward at Joe as she held the dog with a choke chain. Joe, acting quickly, inserted his thumbs into the dog's mouth keeping the dog from clamping down on his fingers. With the dog literally choking, Joe went through his spiel constantly looking at the woman's chest in her negligee. I just laughed like hell at the scene. Also funny was Joe's reference to the "Aviglanese Hall" as the "Vigilante Hall" or the meeting when a comical looking fellow walked to the microphone and introduced himself as Wilson Munez. Joe asked for his address and Wilson answered P.O. Box 167. The crowd really broke up at his reply. Another time was when Joe was answering a woman's question and referred to her as Madam to which she really yelled and stated something like, "I ain't no Madam, I don't sell my body!" I lovingly remember Joe's mother who with failing eyesight always knew me as we talked. She stated she knew it was me because of my size. She said I blocked the sun and light so "she knew it was Peter."

Joe sustained by his intelligence and vitality which clearly enabled him to serve three terms at a time when Port Chester was going through the throes of very bleak days. The rioting in Port Chester from minority factions, the seemingly non-profitable future of the Village that brought deficits to budgets, and a very stagnant Main Street with it's empty stores all added to Joe's woes as Mayor.

JOSEPH P. CARLUCCI
Village Trustee 1974-1977

There appeared on the political scene in 1974 a young candidate for office destined for bigger things politically. This man was Joe Carlucci. An aspiring and gifted attorney, then employed by Dom Pierro, he also served on the staff of Senator Joseph Pisani. His run for a Village Trustee against two entrenched and popular Democratic Trustees (F. Fidelibus and C. Schmehl) was thought by many political experts to be the wrong time. There were those in Republican hierarchy who privately moaned and groaned over Joe's candidacy. They felt he had a promising political career and it would never come to fruition because his chances of winning were very slim. After a two-year hiatus, as the mayoralty candidate who many Port Chester residents were dismayed by his not running in 1972, things didn't look too good for the Republicans. The one thing that no one really thought about or had determined was the almost fanatical way Joe Dzaluk campaigned and ran for office. His enthusiasm carried over to his two running mates. It was also the first time that Dan LaDore and myself co-chaired a political campaign. In our four years in elected office and involvement in previous campaigns, we had learned much and applied our great skills to this seemingly losing campaign. While our three candidates campaigned vigorously, the other side, the Democrats, seemed to be taking the attitude that the Village of Port Chester would follow tradition and would be elected to continue the Democratic majority on the Village Board, expounding on the budget problems while the three Republicans campaigned enthusiastically, especially door to door and outmatched the Democrats.

The Industrial Development Agency, a tool to bring Port Chester into the forefront of change, was expounded on. We showed how the Democrats failed to apply any activity to using the agency. Joe Carlucci, in his bringing out the IDA issue, plus the Carlucci name in Republican politics, started to change the electorate. Towards the end of our campaign at our traditional rally at the Aviglanese Hall, the mood was upbeat, and the Republican Party felt Joe Carlucci would win over Carl Schmehl, Joe Dzaluk had an outside chance to beat Dom Bambace. Bill Davidson was no way a winner.

The final tally on Election Day, 1974, showed the three Republicans victors; a big upset.

Joe Carlucci chose to only serve one three-year term as Trustee and became an expert in IDA financing. He left the firm of Dom Pierro. Joe has a promising career as an attorney and is with the prestigious firm of Cuddy and Feder. His swan song, on his last meeting in office, in a joint statement with Bill Davidson, who also chose not to run again, was a parting shot that infuriated some Republican Party members. Their statements as to the Village Manager being "blind sided" was, as one looks back, true in most instances. With a 4-3 Democratic majority in 1977, Joe Dzaluk was at a real disadvantage as Mayor, yet some of his actions I carried over to my administration also being a minority Mayor in 1986-1988

JOSEPH RENDE
Village Trustee 1989-1992

When Joe Rende was elected Village Trustee, there was one individual who took especially great pride and pleasure in his victory. That was Joe's dad, Anthony Rende. As I stated in the chapter on Tony Rende, the joy and love that showed so strikingly at Joe's swearing in as a Trustee was truly magnificent.

In the three years that was Joe served as a Village Trustee, you could easily sense that Joe Rende was indeed his father's son. His sympathetic concern for those who needed help was a joy to behold. His energies saw to it that quality of life programs such as Port Chester Day, Halloween-in-the-Park, and Christmas and Santa Claus at the Gazebo continued most successfully. It was a tribute to Joe and the Rende family in wanting to see a better Port Chester and to achieve a togetherness of all Port Chester citizens. Joe played an important role in seeing to it that these programs continued and expanded in the number of people who attended. He worked extremely hard as either Chairman or Co-Chairman of these events. On several occasions Sam Terenzi ridiculed Joe for his efforts on behalf of these projects, but Joe merely let these comments not faze him as he continued to work diligently to improve the programs. The irony of Sam's comments was that he always tried to be in attendance at these events.

We suspected that it was not to contribute to their success but merely to be seen and take some credit or praise for efforts he did not contribute to, but accepted with a smile.

As with any elected official, we all have certain flaws that some way lead to our downfall or gives a perception that the electorate views as a total weakness. In my opinion, Joe's flaw was that he placed such strong faith in his best friend, Gary Gianfrancesco. There were some of us, including Republicans, who felt that Joe Rende was led around by Gary on certain volatile issues. If at any time it seemed Gary might have put his foot in his mouth by some statement, Joe Rende would be the first one from the Board to try and clarify Gary's remarks. He was always trying to make Gary look good. Unfortunately, that was not the same case if Joe made a boo-boo. Quite the contrary.

If Joe somehow made a statement and it could be perceived as politically harmful, Joe was left out there all alone.

Joe's whole attitude I guess changed with the vote regarding Willie Marino's application for a car wash permit.

Throughout the long and tedious months before a vote was to be taken on Willie Marino's permit, Willie personally told me he felt by his conversations with Joe that he (Joe) would vote to approve the car wash permit. This, plus the fact that Joe gave such plaudits to Willie and the Marino family at a public hearing, was also a very strong indication that his vote was for Willie's permit. When the vote was taken that evening, Joe's vote was a no vote for the car wash permit. The question will always be on my mind, were the no votes really against Willie Marino or against Mayor Iasillo who supported the project very vocally? It was interesting to note that Joe's comments to the press mirrored Gary Gianfrancesco's. This vote clearly started the further comments of several Board members to start to denigrate, insult, and embarrass me. As I perceived back in the media story in December 1989, and as commented by Dom Pierro in the story, "The organization (Republican) is Crumbling."

As the year 1990 started, Sam Terenzi became more vocal. Privately the other Republican Party Board members were not happy with him. He intimidated them so much that they remained mute. One thing was certain when the Mayor and his ideas or policies came forward; they seemed to unite against the Mayor. It was then that I understood the term, "whipping boy." The 1990 election was won by Branca and Gianfrancesco. The surprising thing, that was a complete revelation to me, was that in a political caucus after the election, John and Gary pushed for Fritz Tedesco, the Port Chester Conservative Party Chairman to sit in on the planning Commission. Fritz Tedesco was instead put on the Taxi Commission, a lesser prestigious commission.

The year 1990 for Joe Rende was a year that Joe didn't involve himself in openly voicing his opinions on various issues. The strain between he and Sam Terenzi was starting to boil over. One issue especially vexing and led to complete disharmony was the question of computerizing the Village Garage. The garage foreman, Dom Tammaro, felt the idea concocted by Terenzi and Giorgi, was merely personal based on the fact that Tammaro ended his personal business relations with Terenzi as his accountant. Rende stepped into the fray on the side of Tammaro. Giorgi, who by now was an ardent supporter of Terenzi, went after Rende. From this came the marriage of Terenzi and Giorgi against Joe Rende. John Branca made tepid remarks regarding the issue. Gianfrancesco was silent as was Colangelo. The garage issue was a prime example of a Republican Party falling apart. What was predicted was now happening.

1991 came, and Joe Rende would now be Deputy Mayor. While other members of the Board continued their attacks on the Mayor, Joe Rende, as Deputy Mayor, was to my way of thinking a good Deputy Mayor. He became more vocal and more knowledgeable of our Village needs. His support of the Volunteer Ambulance Corps, the various celebrations, the Robert Martin Project, all pointed to the maturing of a Trustee. With the quitting of Terenzi and Giorgi from the GOP Party, Joe's chances for re-election dimmed. The election was marked in a survey made by the GOP before the election that stated the GOP candidates should distance themselves from the Mayor. They did, and lost horribly. But, of course, to find a scapegoat, they blamed me and some of my housing attempts, both senior and affordable, as the reasons for their loss. It was almost comical to watch the party point fingers at each other. The Republicans were now as the Democrats were for over a half dozen years, in disarray and getting worse.

I remained silent but attempted to bring the leaders together, however, the remarks from the Board members continued. Joe Rende gracefully took his loss very professionally. Still a young man, I feel Joe might again attempt to run for public office.

MICHAEL D. PIERRO
Village Trustee 1977-1979

When Mike Pierro, along with John Connolly, scored an impressive election victory over Peter Gianukakis and Archie Drago, the scene was now set for the Democratic Party to assume the leadership on the Village Board with John McCrory running the show and Joe Dzaluk a minority Mayor. This indeed did not present a pleasant picture for Mayor Dzaluk, Trustee LaDore, and myself. No one really could guess how loyal Mike Pierro was to the Democratic Party and certain high level Democrats. There were times that the discussions at closed Executive Sessions became rather loud as Mike expounded on his beliefs that party loyalty and party patronage was essential to good government. Dan LaDore and I saw cracks coming from the Democratic majority, most especially through Mike. To his credit, Mike was the type of person who let us all know where he stood on any topic. He surely let John McCrory know how he felt, especially as regards Village Manager, Mike Ritchie, and a call for more patronage. But other matters arose that put Mike and John McCrory at odds with each other, one of which was the appointment of Georgia Kramer to fill a vacant Associate Justice seat. On the surface Mike showed lukewarm support for Ms. Kramer, who did not live in the Village and by Charter could not serve. With the outcry from the concerned citizens group headed by Sal Lucente, Ms. Kramer submitted a letter stating that she would not accept the

Associate Justice seat. The talk around was that Mike led the charge against her appointment.

There was also the proposal to convert the Capitol Theater into a showcase rock nightclub to be named "The Agora Ballroom." At one particularly hot, summer evening where it seemed that the wisdom on the part of the Democrats was probably to accept the idea, Mike was particularly vocal against the idea, which precipitated a bitter vocal exchange between Mike and Ray Sammarco, a member of the Executive Committee of the Village Savings Bank. Regarding this Capitol Theater proposal, I felt Mike was right in questioning the Agora proposal as not being right for Port Chester.

Mike throughout his short term on the Board of Trustees did not propose any great legislation, which by the way, most Trustees never did. Most times the Board is a re-acting group that follows up complaints by their constituency. But I think most people who follow the political scene in Port Chester will remember Mike Pierro and the question associated with his residency in New Jersey while a Trustee.

The question came up late in the final part of Mike's three-year term. With important issues coming before the Board, Mike's absence presented an embarrassment to Mayor McCrory and the Democrats. His being against a proposal to create a post of General Foreman, urged by both Mayor McCrory and Mike Ritchie, was a real blow to the McCrory administration. Mike was against it mostly because of his irritation with the Village Manager. For approximately five months, Mike left the Board on tender hooks as to whether or not he would resign. At one meeting his resignation from the Board was on the agenda and Mike surprised everyone by having it removed at the last minute.

While Mike's resignation brought relief to the Democratic Board, it also created a 3-3 Board and the hope of appointing someone to fill Mike's seat was virtually impossible. Mike really resigned on September 4, 1979. We all knew he had not only business obligations but also marital problems. His resignation was signed "the Honorable Michael D. Pierro." In the past ten years I think I have seen Mike two times. His appearance hadn't changed. He still had the dark glasses and wavy hair and mustache that gave a certain dapper look to his appearance. He created no friends at THE DAILY ITEM because he had the courage to speak his mind which the media objects to.

Right or wrong, Mike Pierro told it straight and true with no baloney. I think I will especially remember him for that.

JOSEPH MUTINO
Village Trustee 1985-1988

It was quite evident that by the mid 1980's the Port Chester Democratic Party had problems. With the exception of Nick Fusco, seemingly unbeatable, the Democrats were frustrated, couldn't raise a great amount of money for their campaigns, and were disorganized. In 1985, Joe Mutino came on the scene. A former Village Engineer with a large Port Chester family was a big advantage but most important was his ability to organize an election campaign. Here was the classic battle, two Italian-Americans going against two non Italian-Americans. It was evident from the start that the Republicans were in for a battle. Although Ray Hellman, a Republican and highly qualified incumbent was up for re-election, there were those Republican leaders who still couldn't take to Ray.

Many of them were also good buddies with Joe Mutino. The question of how hard to work in the campaign for Ray and Dick Cuddy was talked about. When the dust of the 1985 campaign had cleared, it showed Nick Fusco the victor with a 760-vote plurality and Joe Mutino with a 484-vote plurality. Both were impressive numbers. The loss by the Republicans didn't recognize the hard work and organization Joe Mutino brought to the Democrats. The Republicans finally woke up and noticed it after they again lost in the 1986 campaign.

From the very beginning Joe Mutino was going to make his presence known on the Board. His resignation as Village Engineer some time before the election, in which there was talk the Mayor "engineered" this resignation, cropped up and was to play a determining factor in how Joe acted as a Board member. Throughout Joe's campaign, he continually referred to the poor development, especially on Midland Avenue, with too many warehouses and not enough offices. I had determined that after Joe's win I would earnestly work with him because I was the only one who recognized his potential to be a force within the Democratic Party. The first really big vote for Joe came on the night of a really angry gathering of Yacht Club members at a public meeting to decide whether the Board should go ahead to seek plans for the Fox Island site. The gathering was like an "MGM" movie. It was hot that evening with over 100 Yacht Club members yelling and shouting, holding up signs and placards. When another vote was taken, the Board caucused. Joe finally let us know what he needed to vote positively on the resolution. The vote came down to a favorable 6 to 1 vote with Nick Fusco voting no. Joe and I showed agreement on the Robert Martin Co. throughout 1985-1986, but differed on hiring a new Village Engineer. That's the way it went with all issues until the 1986 election when Joe, through his campaign skills and the crusading efforts and hard work of Sapione and Coletti brought a 4 to 3 Democratic majority on the Board. Joe now became the majority leader. The Coastal Zone Management Committee I formed was disbanded. The new committee that was formed consisted of almost everyone I had appointed. It was also at this time that Sapione and Coletti gave the Village Board, the Democrats, and Joe Mutino a headache.

I believe this was the turning point in Joe's attitude towards me. I found us working more closely together. It was also at this time that the two Democrats, Joe and Nick Fusco, realized the Corporation Counsel must go. He did so by resigning. Joe and I went to HUD in Washington, D.C., to put in place the $4.7 million dollar HUD grant. By September 1986, Joe was again having problems as Coletti and Sapione called for Joe's ouster from the Democratic Party. From that point on it seemed Joe and I agreed more and more on the development of Port Chester. We then realized our ideas were closely the same. By the 1987 election, it was politics again as Joe directed Nick Fusco's campaign against me for Mayor. It was a pretty nasty campaign. I defeated Nick by 433 votes and the Open Government candidate by 1,297 votes. After the 1987 election, the number one issue in Port Chester was development. With Joe Coletti now realizing that to keep his alliance with Vinny Sapione was wrong, the Board was solidly now 6-1 for the Robert Martin Plan, the Jim Harvie Plan, the Yacht Club case, and the North Main Street Revitalization.

With Joe Mutino and myself attending conferences and having like professions in the business industry, a closer friendship started between the Mutinos and the Iasillos. Everything was set for the 1988 election that would pit Nick Fusco and Joe Mutino against the Republican slate of Brien McMahon and Sam Terenzi. The smart money was on Fusco and Mutino, but something unheard of happened. Joe decided that three years on the Board of Trustees was enough. He decided not to seek re-election. Many Republicans were elated as were many Democrats because Joe had also irritated some of the Democratic leaders because of his perceived close friendship with the Village Manager. Why did Joe decline to run? I believe, because of several personal reasons. He had a family of two small children, health problems in his family, and his business was just starting to move forward. The question asked many times is if Joe stayed in the race with Nick Fusco, would the Democrats have won? I can't give an answer to that except to say that it would have been a hell of a campaign.

NICK FUSCO
Village Trustee 1972-1988

Webster's Dictionary describes a popular person as one who is widely approved or admired, suitable for the common people, easily comprehended. This really describes Nick Fusco, a Village trustee for 16 years whose popularity and drawing power at elections seemed unbeatable. Nick, a lifelong friend, was to my way of thinking, a throwback to 1960-1970 politicos whose efforts on the Village Board were geared towards taking care of all the personal problems of his constituency. Not giving too much thought to effecting new legislation.

Was this wrong? I really can't say. However, his seemingly formidability at election time made many of those who ran against him shy away from attacking his record and votes on many critical issues.

From his stationary store on Bowman Avenue, Nick had the really tough task of listening each day to legitimate and/or foolish gripes of his constituency, taking advice from many malcontents that I think obscured his ideas, especially in the latter part of his service on the Board of Trustees.

Nick's temper got him in many verbal tussles but somehow he maintained and won his elections.

His thoughts on Village government varied tremendously. Examples of this were his fervent objections to Village Manager/Council type of

161

government for Port Chester, yet in the twilight of his political career, he defended the concept with fervent backing. He voted against an Industrial Development Agency early in his first term, yet later accepted it as the economic hope of the Village. I really feel that many of his votes were made by his feelings that he had to vote with his Democratic Trustees out of a sense of loyalty to the Democratic Party. Ironically, he was never registered as a Democrat. There were many times at Board meetings that he showed he was not fully concerned with some legislation, especially if it concerned financing. However, when it came to problems of the "little guy" such as poor pickup of garbage, dirty streets, full stop signs, traffic lights, etc., Nick Fusco was the guy who understood their dilemma and saw to it that effective action was taken to remedy a problem. On that level, Nick Fusco was the best there was.

One funny incident that sticks in my mind was the problem of parking associated with Cottage Street. It seemed to be that every six months the PARKING, NO PARKING, NO STANDING signs on Cottage Street had to be changed. It in fact became a joke on the Village Board every time requests from neighbors or Village Trustees came forward for sign changes. There were feuds by families on the street that precipitated these sign change requests, and it seemed that the Board would never resolve their problems. At one particular meeting, it became such a folly to continue changing these signs that Nick jokingly suggested putting up flip signs, as they have at football games that denote the downs.

The Board then broke out in uproarious laughter, for it was at this time we recognized how foolish our actions, in the past, regarding this street had been.

If Nick was virtually unbeatable, how did he lose his Trustee re-election in 1988? I think it was for various reasons, one of which primarily was the seemingly poor Democratic organization.

Their effectiveness waned for several years. It showed dramatically in the 1988 election. The year before, Nick was convinced to run against me for Mayor. I thought at the time that it was not a wise move on Nick's part because we both had the same friends and it meant they had to choose to vote between Nick and myself, and I believe my incumbency gave me the advantage. The campaign was unusually dirty. I was particularly, personally attacked by both Nick and Monroe Mann and it truly left a bad taste in my mouth because Nick had followed bad advice and almost ruined our life-long friendship. Today, Nick is out of politics and working in White Plains after selling his store. He genuinely seems happy with his life. His tenure on the Board of Trustees may seem to some as a waste of time, but to me Nick provided the Board with a caring and responsiveness to the "little guy" that perhaps we as Board members sometimes forget.

There is one thing I must relate to, in closing on Nick Fusco. He made my life complete over 45 years ago when he helped in introducing me to my lovely wife, Gloria.

RAYMOND P. HELLMAN
Village Trustee 1981-1985

Some of the qualities I feel are most needed by an elected official are loyalty; loyalty to his Village first and then to the leadership on the Board and to the Mayor, and also to be fully prepared to listen and vote on those issues necessary to make his community develop and prosper. In 1981, such a person who had these qualities was Ray Hellman. I rank Ray as number one in the Trustee category along with Felix Fidelibus. Ray was loyal, but to a point. He would not let his loyalty to the Mayor cloud any of the issues before the Board. There was one trait Ray possessed and that was his ability to break down the most difficult problems to the smallest degree, always thinking ahead of what the consequences would be for future Port Chester citizens on any vote he would make.

Ray would take the time to discuss with the Mayor agenda items before meetings so that he could convey to me how he felt on any important issue and listen to reasons as to why I was for or against an issue.

Never have I, to this day, seen any Trustee who was so prepared when a Board meeting commenced.

He had memos, letters, and documents, all categorized and filed in such an order that if any problem arose during a discussion, Ray Hellman had the facts and figures in front of him and imparted to all very succinctly his knowledge as to what was discussed, debated, and voted on at previous meetings. To

164

some on the Board there was a feeling that Ray was grandstanding, especially when he would, in a clear, concise manner, speak using a vocabulary that was definitely not understandable by some Board members and the audience. Those Board members who repudiated Ray, behind his back, were actually very jealous of him and of his superiority with both his vocabulary and common sense. It eventually caused them to try to downgrade his excellence on the Board to Republican Party regulars. As I look back to those early 1980's when things were falling into place and the Village was getting better publicity, there quietly arose by some Board members some secret agendas, one of which was to deflate the Mayor and the publicity I was garnering. The ugly head of jealousy was now coming to the forefront.

It was almost comical to see some members of the audience come forward and ask questions or issue statements regarding Village policy. With any meeting, I determined that if I answered every question or debated every issue, there would be a feeling imparted that I was trying to grandstand. I implored the Republican Board members to speak out. In a sense, this was also a way of protecting my backside. Only one Trustee would listen to my plea, Ray Hellman. As Deputy Mayor, he intelligently interceded on many issues. His vocabulary was fantastic. There were many meetings that Ray would answer a question and you could see the citizen who asked the question leave the microphone with a dazed, quizzical look on his face. The truth was Ray always spoke that way. It wasn't a put-on. Getting to know Ray in his years on the Board also indicated to me he had a "British" type of humor, say on the David Niven style that cracked me up. His humor, not understandable by his so-called Republican backers, I feel also helped to defeat Ray in 1985. However, when one, after many years, analyzes that 1985 election, the following was apparent. Ray in 1985 was running with a fellow candidate, Richard Cuddy, who campaigned in a style that didn't seem to excite the electorate.

Ray was running against Nick Fusco, an acknowledged successful vote getter and Joe Mutino, a former Village Engineer and a young American-Italian with a large family in Port Chester.

When you add to this the fact heard around town that Republican friends of Joe Mutino out of some disjointed loyalty did not campaign for Ray, you had all the ingredients for a Republican defeat.

Ray took his defeat gracefully, having good common sense to leave politics and not ever consider running again for public office. As Chief Executive Officer, it was my pleasure later on to appoint Ray to the Port Chester Housing Authority where he continued to operate efficiently and with great dedication. My thoughts of Ray Hellman are, as Ray might state it, his tenure in office was one of great repute.

While his conduct was viewed by some as repugnant, his representation as a Village Trustee was clearly considerable and notable. In other words, Ray Hellman was an excellent member of the Board of Trustees.

We have become good friends and his loyalty to me continues.

RICHARD GIORGI
Village Trustee 1989-1992

Rick Giorgi came upon the political scene literally by accident. Although an Independent, Rick worked diligently on several election campaigns for Republicans and was active in Port Chester with several service clubs. In the year he was approached to run, there was some doubt as to whether or not he would accept the Republican nomination. He had plans to move to North Carolina and sell his florist business so there was hesitancy as to accepting. At the time, however, his business was in a decline. As a result, it made the sale of the business difficult. The Republican Party knew of this but they first had to find a candidate to run with Joe Rende, and if the candidate (Rick) won and still felt he wanted to move to North Carolina, the Board, solidly Republican, would appoint someone to fill the seat.

In the campaign with Rende and Giorgi for Trustees and myself for Mayor, they asked advice, opinions, and direction on how to campaign. The Mayor was the veteran campaigner, a leader, the person who could raise large sums of money for the campaign. But as soon as they made it, running on the Mayor's leadership and ideas and the attitude of "we're behind you 100%, Mayor" was forgotten. As they became Trustees, it became a different ballgame. It was the same with Rick and others that I helped. Sometimes being behind the Mayor 100% meant they were in a better position to stab him in the back.

The campaign over, we all won. We ran on specific issues that were highlighted and campaigned on, yet when victory came, it seemed the young Trustees forgot it all. They say the elderly forget and develop a sort of Alzheimer's disease. Such was not the case in Port Chester.

The young Trustees forgot pledges and resorted, eventually, to what I call plain old politics.

Rick had all the potential to be a very valuable Trustee in our Village, but somehow he fell under the spell of Sam Terenzi and eventually the grand puppeteer, Fritz Tedesco. Fritz waited years and he finally pulled into his ultra-right Conservative Party two Trustees who were hell-bent on taking over politics and government in Port Chester. It was somewhat amazing that when Rick became a Trustee, his confidence level with me was extremely high, but as with most immature people, he began to strike out. With his Buddy, Sam Terenzi, they started what would be in less than three years, the downfall of the very successful Port Chester Republican Party. You could sense the division in the ranks of the Republican Board happening day by day. Terenzi with his intimidating manner and Gianfrancesco with his sights on bigger political treasures pulled in Giorgi and the downfall of the Republican Party began.

I suppose the big issues that motivated Rick's allegiance to Terenzi were code enforcement, the budget, and a somewhat disillusionment with Village Manager Mike Ritchie. It would seem that when there were matters that upset Terenzi and Giorgi and somehow Mike Ritchie by logic and proof showed their approach to these matters completely wrong. They then figured that Ritchie was somehow listening to me, which was totally wrong. As a result, if I sided with Mike Ritchie, it only made the two Trustees angrier and more dedicated to crucifying me. For 18 months the Republican Party was engulfed in fights and quarrels. The 1992 election clearly showed that the Republican Party had hit bottom. Terenzi, months before the election, defected from the GOP, followed by Giorgi and the downhill spiral accelerated faster. The issue of affordable housing was pressed forward by Terenzi and Giorgi and when they received an important assist by Gianfrancesco, the downhill spiral really now spiraled at a maddening pace.

The 1992 election saw both Rende and Giorgi lose. Rick's loss was most painful because he lost by one vote. I feel quite positive that Rick Giorgi, if he doesn't move out of Port Chester, will again run for office. Will it be as a Trustee or Mayor? Who can predict that, only time will tell.

ROBERT KANCIR
Village Trustee 1979-1983

One of the first things you learn on entering the political field is that you can't win an election unless you have the support of one of the two major parties, Democrat or Republican. One person who successfully debunked that theory was Bob Kancir in a special election held in 1979. When Mike Pierro resigned from his Trustee seat, it created a Board of Trustees of three Democrats and three Republicans. As a result, the names brought forward to serve out Pierro's term never got the necessary four votes for an appointment. The stage was set for a December 6, 1979 special election pitting Republican Joe Dzaluk, former Mayor, against Democrat Joe Guarino who had lost in the regular 1979 spring election to Dan LaDore by one vote. However, one other name entered the campaign and that was Bob Kancir, a registered Republican who ran on the Conservative-Independent Citizen's line. The campaign was not really spectacular because all three candidates supported redevelopment, Village Manger Law, and more recreational programs. However, Bob had an edge because there was a feeling prevalent in the community that there was too much politics being played on the Village Board. Bob received a hefty endorsement from THE DAILY ITEM, picture included, supporting his candidacy. As a result, what many thought would not happen, did happen. Bob Kancir, with a dedicated force of people, won that special election handily. As a result of Bob's victory, there was extreme pressure put on him to cast his one vote at meetings for either Republican or Democratic issues and programs.

Bob started slowly and carefully as a new Trustee listening very closely to all discussions. There were many who thought his ideas and decisions were being orchestrated by Conservative Party Chairman, Fritz Tedesco. What this meant was that any time any discussion came up regarding new housing projects for low to middle income citizens, Bob's vote would be a negative one. After four months in office at the next general election, Bob by law had to run again for his seat. In an election which saw me best Mayor McCrory, Bob tallied the second most votes for Trustee after John Connolly, while Carmen Talia came in third to fill the un-expired seat of Dan LaDore. During his next three years as Trustee, I continually sought Bob's support on far-reaching programs I visualized as being important to Port Chester's future. As I had predicted, Bob, even after a meeting with HUD officials and having been told the importance of the Kingsport and Southport Housing Developments, voted no on accepting the programs.

Fortunately supporting me were Trustees Connolly, Repaci, and Talia, and this major program was adopted and went forward.

Throughout Bob's term in office, he received bad advice from his Conservative supporters. His votes on redevelopment, especially in the South Main Street redevelopment, were often erratic in that he might vote against the project yet then vote to condemn the necessary properties on the sites involved. In 1982 he was convinced that the time was right for him to run against me as Mayor. With the Democrats, Conservatives, and Village Independent Parties endorsing him, it seemed to many that a solid backing such as this would guarantee him victory. It didn't turn out that way as I bested Bob by an overwhelming majority. With two strong running mates, Carmen Talia and Brien McMahon, we swept to victory. Bob served out his three-year term and ran for re-election again and lost. There was rumor that the Concerned Citizens Committee was disillusioned with Bob and as a result, did not give him their wholehearted support. Bob after that never stayed active in politics until my fourth term when he heartily supported me. Those few years before Bob passed away at a very young age, we became closer. He built up his grocery store business which was being run by his lovely wife Sophie, and son, Andy, and is the hub of Brooksville politics.

While Bob served he showed one important thing to all those politicians who think they know it all, an Independent candidate can indeed win an election in Port Chester. If anything, Bob left as a legacy that fact.

SAVERIO TERENZI
Village Trustee 1988-1993

To say that Sam Terenzi came upon the political scene in 1988 would be too simplistic. Sam Terenzi literally burst upon the political scene. His entering the race was heaven sent for Sam. In the Trustee race he had Brien McMahon leading the ticket, an individual loved and honored by many in Port Chester. Brien was always considered a "good guy." The fact that Trustee Joe Mutino decided not to seek re-election was also favorable to Sam's election. Trustee Nick Fusco, without Mutino directing his campaign hurt him tremendously. The fighting within the Democratic Party hurt Vin Sapione and his endorsement on Monroe Mann for Trustee on an Indpendent line. All these factors plus a Republican Party that was rich in campaign funds, hard working district leaders and a Republican administration that showed the failings of the Democratic majority for two years, blended together to bring a great victory for McMahon and Terenzi.

Sam Terenzi, from the beginning, was aggressive in his way to get what he felt was in the best interests of the Village. However, there were those who looked askance at the way he operated.

He got his lawyer, Will Stephens appointed as Corporation Counsel and also intimidated Board members by removing Tony Bellantoni from the Planning Commission. There were only McMahon and myself who questioned the Republican Party's wisdom at this move but in order to not start out in a belligerent manner, party district leaders caved in to Terenzi's demands. It's ironic that Terenzi's first words as a Trustee at his first Board meeting were, "I think we've got a real team here." Years later, history will show that Terenzi was the person that almost ruined the Republican Party; "the team."

In Terenzi's first term, many problems came forward. The Yacht Club, the continuance of the Landmark Ethics hearing, Robert Martin, the group home on West Street, and many other issues showed the seemingly vociferous Terenzi very quiet. It wasn't until January 1989, eleven months after being sworn in as a Trustee that he opened up.

In two inspections at 2 Drew Street and 51 Grove Street, during a particularly cold winter, building inspectors found overcrowding at these buildings. Trustee Terenzi, in his "solicitous" fashion, didn't care about the weather and just kicked out the tenants that overcrowded these buildings.

Then in March 1989, he supported having a police commissioner over a police chief. He liked the idea because as he stated, "The commissioner, if he mouths off or doesn't do his job, can get bounced in a minute." It was evident that now with a year under his belt as Trustee, Sam was starting to bellow and roar. In May 1989 on an overcrowding issue, he made truly embarrassing remarks about me. Ridiculing my efforts for creating quality of life programs was, in fact, stopping the effectiveness of inspections on the overcrowding issue.

The car wash vote for Willie Marino was, I believe, the crowning achievement for Sam Terenzi. His marshalling enough votes to turn down this project would later be shown to be the downfall of the Republican Party. By now, Terenzi was also having his own financial problems.

With the election of Rick Giorgi as a Trustee, Terenzi found the perfect ally and person to go forward in seeking ways many believed not to improve the Village but to improve their own political lives. The 1990 budget talks really brought them in conflict with the other Board members. It was evident that they in no way would try to seek a compromise on any issues. Their volatile arguments against purchasing a leaf vacuum machine, the question of the Village garage and its foreman, Dom Tammaro, in keeping records, the Village Manager's capabilities, all ironically gave headlines to Terenzi who often criticized me for seeking headlines.

In 1991, the election drew near. I was seeking a sixth term, Terenzi a second term, and Dan Colangelo his first term since being appointed. It was quite evident to all political sages that Terenzi, having Iasillo and Colangelo leading the ticket with somewhat weak Democratic candidates, stood a good chance to win. The knowledgeable political people were right. Terenzi won by a mere 205 votes. When judged against the Democrats who were financially poor, unorganized, and without a mayoralty candidate, Terenzi was lucky.

As I went forward in my sixth term as Mayor, I realized that with Terenzi and Giorgi and a quiet Dan Colangelo, my term would be rocky, and I then started to seriously consider this to be my last term.

Although we welcomed a fantastic storage building, Westy's, it was evident that the summer of 1991, politically, was to be hectic and horrendous. South Main Street and its redevelopment was facing strong opposition by Terenzi and Giorgi.

Their statements made some Trustees back off and not support a development that would effectively change for the better the face of our Village. Sixty homes proposed by a young Village developer, Louis Larizza, were facing strong opposition. I was also striving to develop a new senior housing development for our Village. After a heated debate, both projects were turned down. The Larizza development was truly sad insofar as Trustee Gianfrancesco, whose vote could have turned the vote around, voted against it.

In December, 1991, Rick Giorgi broke from the GOP, followed weeks later by Sam Terenzi. It was evident that their defections before the budget process were planned to disrupt the Village at budget time. By their defection, it meant Joe Rende had to seek a candidate to run with him in the March election. Jose Santos was chosen by the GOP. The election was a great victory for the Democrats, McCrory and DiRoberto, beating the GOP, and Giorgi, who was outdistanced by one vote.

Now with Terenzi, McCrory, DiRoberto on the Board, the reasons for me not to run for a seventh term became more viable.

Almost immediately, with the new coalition aided and abetted by Gianfrancesco and Colangelo, Mike Ritchie was fired.

The theft of tapes from my office made Terenzi bolder and started my second Ethics hearing (See chapter on second Ethics hearing). The Home Depot proposal, thank God, came forward. New York State approved the local water revitalization program, recycling was going forward, and I tried valiantly to seek 2:00 A.M. bar closings in our Village. The Port Chester Planning Office Reorganization created headlines for Terenzi. It was amazing. The Mayor had to answer Terenzi's absurdities while the rest of the Board remained very quiet.

Towards mid-December 1992, I announced that I would not seek a seventh term. It was amazing how Terenzi stated, "Personally, I never had a problem with him. I like him."

"

THERESA REPACI
Village Trustee 1978-1981

By a very close vote, by a margin of eight votes, Theresa Repaci won her election over Joseph Poletsky, a retired police lieutenant. Her plurality was viewed by some as small because of the huge loss of Dan LaDore who unsuccessfully ran for Mayor against John McCrory. Theresa was an active Republican Party member who was intelligent, active, and at times, showed a temper to match any person, male or female. She became the second woman ever to hold public office in Port Chester, the first being Marion Kastrud. There was a certain priority that Dan LaDore and I viewed as Theresa's main concern. This was her unyielding support for a strong manager form of government which sometimes put her at loggerhead with Dan and me. Because of the fact Dan LaDore was starting to show the effects of cancer, he started missing meetings. As a result, it was up to Theresa and me to carry the Republican banner at Board meetings. There were several times we disagreed with each other. As a result, there were those in the Republican Party who felt because of my seniority on the Board, Theresa should have supported me more. It didn't turn out that way because they, the Republican Party, failed to realize that Theresa had a mind of her own and to her credit, displayed it on numerous occasions. I thought her actions and votes at times were wrong, however, I respected her firmness of conviction.

One such incident of her toughness was at a meeting of over 150 neighbors at a meeting at Horton School on a hot summer evening. While Mayor McCrory and the entire Board were aware of the meeting, only Theresa appeared, due to the fact that the rest of the Board was in Executive Session. As a result, she bore the brunt of the evening's yelling and screaming by a restless crowd made up of mostly residents of Weber Drive Housing Project and other low-income housing advocates. I still feel that her vote to approve a disco nightclub at the Capitol Theater was wrong. Her seemingly 100% support of Village Manager actions was also not right in my mind. However, in retrospect, as one looks back to those years Theresa served as a Trustee, she was under extreme pressure because she was a woman. In today's politics, women seeking public office or serving in public office is normal and regarded as a monumental step; however, in those late 1970's it was a different story. Theresa only chose to serve one term of three years and stepped down in 1981. While her term was not spectacular, she proved that by her firmness and strength a woman could indeed serve. Her greatest triumph was probably convincing the Board of Trustees to approve a first home in Port Chester for retarded citizens on King Street. In the past ten years, Theresa and I have only met once, at a summer concert in the park where her mom, Jean Viglatto, received a Community Service Award. Theresa seemed happy in her new professional life. I feel her three years on the Board helped her to take on any other situations that would pop up in her life.

VINCENT SAPIONE
Village Trustee 1986-1989

In the mid 1980's the Village of Port Chester was literally locked in combat with the Port Chester Yacht Club regarding the 20-year lease the Yacht Club had with the Village. Things really got rough as statements from both sides appeared in the newspapers. I received many phone calls early in the morning which. When I picked up the phone I was told, "You ain't going to be in office long," or "You're finished, Mayor." My wife even received a call questioning her about our granddaughter and her school schedule, which really terrified us. Things got very scary.

The upcoming election for the two Trustee seats in 1986 became important because a Democratic victory for the two seats would give the Democrats a majority on the Village Board, and I would become the minority Mayor.

The Democrats put forward two young Italian-Americans, Vincent Sapione and Joseph Coletti, both yacht Club members, to run against Republican incumbents Brien McMahon and Carmen Talia. It was a tough campaign and the results showed the winners to be Vinny Sapione with a 33 vote plurality and Joe Coletti with an 18 vote plurality. Immediately the political pundits stated the strength of the Yacht Club enabled the Democrats to win. I disputed this. A lethargic attitude by the Republicans, who really did not pull together, lost the election. The Yacht Club issue had nothing to do with the campaign. With their majority now on the Village Board, the Democrats started out with controversial appointments. Their choice for Village Treasurer lived out of Port Chester, and their choice for Corporation Counsel was a citizen who was involved in lawsuits against the Village, but was also the legal representative of the Yacht Club. The Democrats started out with Vin Sapione taking the lead on most issues, by instituting a lawsuit to recover land from a waterfront restaurant the Democrats claimed belonged to the Village. The Waterfront Commission was reformed. But the issue that really set off a Democratic split of Sapione-Coletti versus Mutino-Fusco was the Robert Martin Development Plan. Sapione, along with Coletti and with the advice and prodding I believe of the Corporation Counsel, took out against the RMC Plan with a vengeance completely tearing the Board apart. It was a bitter fight that saw in less than six months the resignation of the Corporation Counsel. The other two Democrats, along with the three Republican Board members, had a resolution ready to fire the Corporation Counsel. However, Sapione evidently heard of this and rather than being fired, the Corporation Counsel resigned. After only six months, the Sapione-Coletti faction was calling for the resignation of Mutino-Fusco from the Democratic Party. Things got to such a state that because of Sapione-Coletti, RMC was seriously considering withdrawal from any development in Port Chester. Then something happened. Joe Coletti recognized the foolishness and the foolhardiness of Sapione and the Yacht Club and changed, thank God.

On all the important development issues Joe united with the Village and Vin Sapione was now alone.

For over two years, Vin Sapione was the negative voice on the Board of Trustees. In 1987, when I was up for re-election, rather than back the Democratic candidate, Nick Fusco, he instead backed the "Open Government Party" candidate, the former Corporation Counsel. This further weakened the Democratic Party. The Democratic Party was now a shell, empty within. After my victory in a rather messy campaign, Vin Sapione then went after me with the Landmark Ethics Case. (This will be covered in a separate statement.) My credibility and good name was at stake. The case dragged on and on. In 1989 Vin Sapione, as the story is related to me, packed the Democratic caucus and was chosen to run against me for the seat of Mayor. This was the perfect opportunity to see if the people of Port Chester believed all of the negative and half truths being spit out by Sapione. The people recognized these falsehoods, and I was re-elected for a fifth term. Sapione was trounced and left the Board and with it went the most negative voice I can ever remember in my 20 years as a public official occupying a seat on the Village Board. In 1990 he tried to recover his Trustee seat and again was trounced. After these two defeats, I feel Vinny Sapione will still try to come back, however, even the Yacht Club seems to have changed their attitudes and ideas, and it might be because of Vinny Sapione's poor representation of many of the facts regarding our waterfront development that may have reversed their thinking.

WILLIAM C. DAVIDSON
Village Trustee 1974-1977

If there ever was an individual who stood possibly the least amount of chance to win an election as a Port Chester Village Trustee, that person was Bill Davidson. It wasn't that Bill didn't have qualifications to serve. Bill's background in real estate law and an inclination to working hard and a sense of honesty and fair play would have made Bill an ideal candidate for office. Except in Port Chester. Many of the so-called political experts gave Bill little or no chance of winning, especially against two incumbents, Felix Fidelibus and Carl Schmehl. From the very start of the campaign, those in the higher up of the Republican Party felt Bill was merely a fill-in candidate, a warm body put in just to fill up the voting line. He was fortunately running with the two Joes, Joe Dzaluk and Joe Carlucci, both well known and from big families in Port Chester. That always helped win an election. Bill Davidson, on the other hand, was known primarily because of his father, an attorney, who for many years was the attorney for the Village Savings Bank. When any mortgages or closings were made on homes for sale through the Savings Bank, Bill's dad was involved. From the beginning of the campaign, Bill was referred to as "what's his name."

Bill's style of campaigning was low-key and his speech making was frequently lack luster. As a result of this and because he was not of Italian ancestry no one even considered him too highly in the campaign. One thing

Bill did possess was his ability to take a joke when it was aimed at him. I vividly remember at our final closing rally at the Aviglanese Hall, for which I was the Master of Ceremonies, I introduced Bill by stating, "Our next speaker is a fellow who entered this campaign not well known, and is frequently referred to as what's his name. Today after weeks of strenuous campaigning, Bill is now recognized and is now referred to as 'Mister' what's his name." At this joke Bill broke up laughing heartily, which became contagious as the jam-packed hall burst out in laughter. The rest is history.

Bill Davidson won his election by 336 votes, a large plurality over strong incumbents, and became a Trustee in spite of what the political experts felt were disadvantages in his campaign. Bill's tenure in office was not a spectacular one, although as the Village's Fire Commissioner he performed admirably and with some distinction. Bill's ability not to be bullied at meetings by constituents was something to behold. At those frequent times when the arguments became rather loud and political, Bill contained himself and answered when questioned, clearly, concisely, and softly. However, a dead giveaway to his demeanor was how his face turned a beet red. Another indication was his fiddling with a large gold watch he would take from his pocket. Bill Davidson chose not to run for a second term. He felt that what he wanted to do was accomplished. That was, to see that the Village Manager/Council form of government was started. His last act as Trustee was a statement he and Joe Carlucci co-authored. It stirred the waters for a short period of time but as usually happens, their statement was heard, read, and then forgotten. I don't see much of Bill Davidson today. While he served his three years as Trustee, his term is probably forgotten and that's a shame because Bill Davidson served not with great publicity, but rather honestly, with quiet dignity and with a fervent attempt at doing what he felt was best for Port Chester.

FRANK "OZZIE" ZUMPANO
Village Trustee 1970-1972

If there ever was an individual that I have admired and respected, it was my political mentor that got me involved in politics in 1970, my good friend, Frank "Ozzie" Zumpano. A former Village Trustee, Police Commissioner, and former Chairman of the Port Chester Republican Party, Ozzie was truly a friend that I looked to for political advice in those early days of my political life. Ozzie was a politician of the late 1960's and early 1970's who campaigned as was dictated by political parties. Namely, passing out palm cards, attending funerals and wakes of everyone, even those people you never knew, being seen at almost every function in every part of the community, and of course, campaigning door to door. Now, attending every function was important, but being seen there was even more important. Ozzie had a method that guaranteed this.

I knew it as the "going to the bathroom" plan. This plan meant that one must attend a function very early and get a seat up front, say, at a concert, and sit in the center. This was very important. I remember the first time I followed the Ozzie Zumpano "going to the bathroom" plan.   We were at a concert at the Port Chester High School, sitting center stage and down front. At the appropriate time, Ozzie turned to me and said, "Go to the bathroom." I replied, "What for?" He answered, "The people will see you as you walk to the back."

I did this by exiting from the left side and after intermission I did the same thing exiting from the right side. I'm sure many people saw Peter Iasillo at the concert.

Another Ozzie Zumpano plan was to have your name announced on the loud speaker at various events. Now, do these sort of things guarantee victory at the polls? I don't know, but I was elected in 1970 with a very impressive plurality. With this victory I now had the opportunity to serve on the Village Board with Ozzie. Ozzie won his election in 1969 against a strong Democratic incumbent candidate and became Port Chester's Police Commissioner, a title and job he relished, loved, and worked at with vigor and vitality.

Unfortunately, Ozzie was continuously laughed at behind his back. But there was never a human being who served Port Chester with such honesty and love.

There was a time on the Board when Ozzie was about to make a public statement. However, before the meeting, Ozzie ate figs, and seeds from the figs were stuck between Ozzie's palate and his false teeth. The result, rather than a reasonably literate statement, became a series of mumbling that brought laughter to many in attendance.

Frank "Ozzie" Zumpano was not a great speaker, was not blessed with the ability to debate, was an individual who only served one term of three years as a Trustee, and probably never introduced a great piece of legislation. However, no one I have served with on the Village Board possessed such love, compassion, and concern for his fellow Port Chesterites more than Ozzie Zumpano. I conclude by relating to 1968 when I suffered three heart attacks and almost died. I was not financially well off, my wife and three children were in a state of shock and wondering what to do with me not at home. The first person to offer help, both financially and lovingly, was Ozzie Zumpano. Ozzie Zumpano was loved by many, many people because he was filled with love and care for so many people in return.

SOME ACCOMPLISHMENTS OF MAYOR IASILLO'S ADMINISTRATION
1980-1993

- Lyon Farm Condominiums
- Village Green Condominiums
- Kings Park Condominiums
- Washington Mews Condominiums
- Landmark Condominiums (Life Savers)
- Southport and Kingsport Housing Developments
- Grieco Cottage Street Rental Housing
- Gateway Office Bldg. (First Office Building in Port Chester in 35 Years)
- Midland Ave. Corporate Park
- Benerofe Office Building
- Baker-Modern Tobacco Office Building
- Westy's Storage Facility.
- Horton School Bldg. Revitalization
- Caldor brought back to Port Chester
- Completion of Landscaping to Caldor Parking Lot
- Simone Shopping Center
- Completion of Village Gateway-Midland Avenue Extension
- Repaved, Illuminated, New Sidewalks, Trees and Circa 1900.

- Lamps for North Main Street Shopping District
- Repaved, Expanded and Illuminated Railroad Station
  Parking Lot
- Encouraged over 350 New Businesses into Port Chester
- Received through Community Development Block grants approx. $8
  Million
- Received through Port Chester Development Corp. over $7
  Million plus 190 New Housing Units
- Received through Section 312 Program, for Lending, for
  Rehabilitation over $4.5 Million, Rehabilitating 26,000 Square feet
  Commercial Space and 235 Housing Unit.
- Loaned through Port Chester UDAG Repayment Façade Program
  $75,000 Interest Free
- Received Coastal Zone Management Funding, $20,000
- Received $500,000 from Federal Gov't for highway repairs as a
  result of the Mianus River Bridge Disaster
- Encouraged through IDA Funding Ten Projects, Issuing Bonds
  Totaling $27.5 Million
- Received Environmental Quality Bond Grant from New York
  State Parks and Recreation, $1.3 Million
- Assisted in the Sale of the Village Savings gateway Office Bldg.
  realizing Payback to the Village of Port Chester of $500,000
  UDAG Funds
- Obtained through Urban Development Block Grants over $20
  Million Both Public and Private Sources.
- From May 1980 to May 1985, witnessed New Construction
  and/or Reconstruction of 485,000 Square feet Residential
  Development, 432,000 Square Feet Retail-Office Development,
  352,000 Square Feet Warehouse-Industrial Development.
- Created Local Waterfront Revitalization Program (LWRP)
- Created Waterfront Commission
- Initiated Senior Nutrition Program at the Don Bosco Center
- Initiated the Christmas Tree Lighting Ceremony in Village
  Square
- Initiated Christmas Caroling and Santa Claus Visit at Lyon Park
- Re-instated Annual Village Home Christmas Decoration Awards
- Initiated "Port Chester Plus" Public Relations Program
- Initiated 6.2 Mile Mini-Marathon, the Bed Races and Bicycle
  Races
- Initiated the Summer Concert Series in Lyon Park
- Instituted the Year End Report Bulletin

- Formed the Port Chester Council of the Arts
- Co-Sponsor of the Annual Byram River Arts Festival
- Created the North Main Street Festival, Re-Dedicating the North Main Street Shopping District
- Erected and Dedicated "Mayor Peter Iasillo Gazebo" at Lyon Park
- Established Two Mini-Sculpture Parks in the North Main Street Shopping District
- Dedicated Memorials to the late Joseph Suppa, Sr., Peter Pergamo and Barry Flynn.
- Initiated Village Field Day Events for Young People (Jr. Olympics).
- Completed Renovation of Historic Bush Homestead
- Erected new "Welcome to Port Chester" Signs
- Illuminated Softball and Baseball Field, in partnership with the Port Chester School Board
- Dedicated the William James Memorial Park, the "Chappie" Posillipo Park and the Argelio Rodriguez Park
- Completed the Landscaping of Civil War Park, Cannon Park, and the Police Station
- Created the Port Chester Youth Bureau
- Created the Drug Free School Zone Program
- Assisted in the Construction of the Port Chester PBA Memorial, Lifesaver Bldg. and the South Main Street Firehouse designated Historical Landmarks
- Established Mayors Award for Boy Scouts
- Established Community Service Awards
- Erected Police Booth in Liberty Square
- Created "Port Chester Day" and "Halloween-in-the-Park" as Annual Events
- Installed, First Time, Black Minister as Assoc. Chaplain for PBA
- Installed, First Time, Physician for the Fire Department
- Established Mayors Award for Outstanding High School Football, Baseball Athletes and Cheerleaders
- Created Position of Full Time Village Attorney and Engineer
- Pathmark Shopping Center
- Initiated Softball Games vs. Soap Opera Stars for Charity,
- Brought to Port Chester "Nadel Industries".
- Complete Renovation of Court Room including New Lighting, Air Conditioning, Sound System, Ceiling, and Seating
- Initiated Bringing Home Depot to Port Chester

ACKNOWLEDGEMENTS

The author would like to thank the following people, who, without their generous help and kindness, this book would not be possible.

- Richard "Fritz" Falanka
- Pamela Palmer Mutino
- Toni Rovella,
- Raymond Hellman
- Brien McMahon
- Goldie Solomon
- Dr. Janusz Richards
- Gloria Iasillo
- Judy Iasillo
- Amanda Iasillo
- Rebecca Iasillo
- Kathy DiMattio
- Stacey DiMattio
- Peter Iasillo, Jr.
- Hon. Michael Borrelli
- Louis Larizza
- Maurice Cueva-Eguiguren
- President Ronald Reagan
- Village of Port Chester Past Elected Officials
- Hope Vespia

THE AUTHOR

Peter Iasillo is a life long resident of Port Chester, New York and a graduate of Port Chester High School. As the Mayor of Port Chester from 1980 to 1993, he served as President of the Westchester County Village Officials Association, as a member of the Policy Committee for Community and Economic Development for the National League of Cities.

He served as a member of the Executive Committee of the New York State Conference of Mayors, as a member of the Town/Village/County Task Force, as a member of the Pace University Advisory Committee for the Conference on Communities. His membership also included the National Conference of Republican Mayors, the Westchester 2000 Board, the Westchester Business Partnership and the County Special Committee on Sales Tax Revenues.

The author's awards are numerous and include the United Cerebral Palsy of Westchester, the Boy Scouts of America, Westchester Community Action, Westchester O.I.C., the American Legion and the Leukemia Society of America. He has been listed in Who's Who in the East and Who's Who in America. He was awarded the prestigious Westchester County Merit Medal.

Married since October 14, 1950 to the former Gloria Sementini, they have three talented offspring, Peter Jr., Kathy, and Judy. With their three grand daughters, Amanda, Stacey, and Rebecca and their son-in-law Pat, the author feels he has the best of all worlds.

Some of the author's other writings include "The Saga of Benny Vinci: A War Hero"; "My Dad, A Short Story of a Genius: Casper Iasillo, Sr."; "Christmas Day: 1994/1934" (a short story); "Growing up in the Bowery and Purdy's Grove Park".

CONCLUSION

After 23 years, I look back and wonder if history will judge my efforts as a public official with disfavor or with honor. I wrote not with venom in my heart, rather, to give a history of a great and wonderful village. There will be those who will perceive this narrative as a "get even" story. Far from it. I praise all those officials I served with for their involvement added to the mystique and wonder of Port Chester. While what I envisioned and related will make some question my sincerity or truth, I wrote what I alone felt in my heart. I will always remember the thrills and excitement of seeing an idea or plan completed successfully. The disappointment of bearing witness to negative votes, while they provided me let down at the time, I now look at as a maturing process. While I viewed it at the time as a personal affront, I now realize that some vote taking was sometimes a game, a political diversion. In years to come, voters hopefully will remember those public officials whose views and votes may have hampered true progress for Port Chester.

What a grand and glorious part of my life. I view in my room all those plaques, pictures, and proclamations and my chest swells as I remember each and every presentation. I remember those many meetings, the thousands I sat through as Trustee and Mayor, and listened, sometimes with excitement, sometimes with sadness, sometimes with pain, and sometimes with boredom.

I shall always remember those citizens who came before the board. Some came with tears as they related their plight, some "smart alecks" tried to trick the board to create arguments in an attempt to gain media attention, and some who came before us whose statement, while sincere, was sometimes so confusing that it required hands put over one's mouth to squelch a laugh.

I shall remember many whose time had come to leave the Village, whose life brought joy to me and many other Village residents. Tears often come to my eyes for they represented a part of my life that I remember. My hope for Port Chester is that those who win elected office will view their public service as a time to honor the Village.

What a wonderful community.

Finally, the question, "Was it worth it?"

You bet it was!

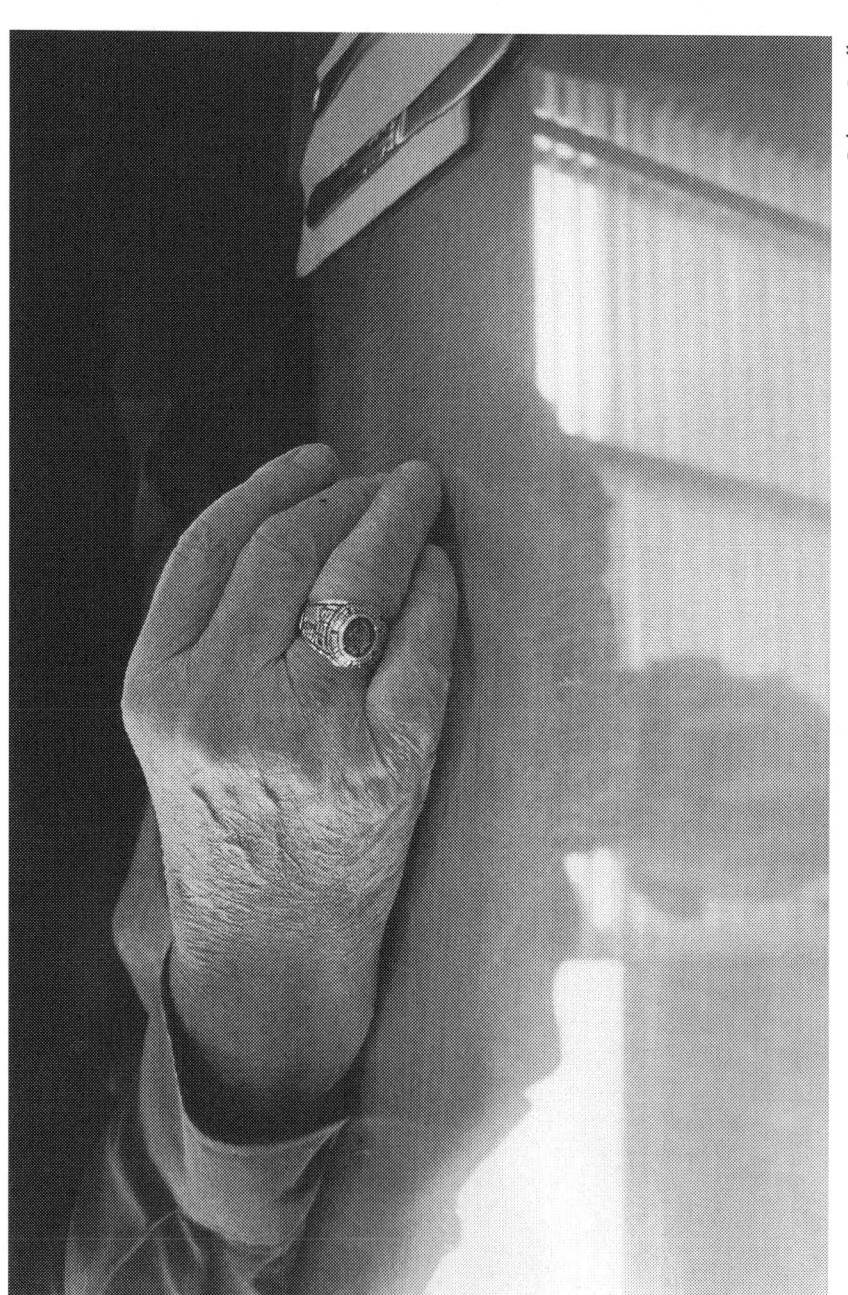